17 HOURS TO MORE CLARITY, COURAGE, AND CONFIDENCE

A REPEATABLE ROADMAP OF INTERMITTENT FASTING, MEDITATING, AND CREATING — OH, BUT YOU DON'T HAVE TO

BRADLEY CHARBONNEAU

"Be miserable. Or motivate yourself. Whatever has to be done, it's always your choice."

— WAYNE DYER

"There are basically two types of people. People who accomplish things, and people who claim to have accomplished things. The first group is less crowded."

— MARK TWAIN

These were both just too good to pass up.

DEDICATION

To those of us who struggled and suffered, whined and moaned, tried and tormented, and thought it was true that we all must write a book, meditate, or intermittent fast.
We don't have to.
But if we want to ...

CONTENTS

PREFACE

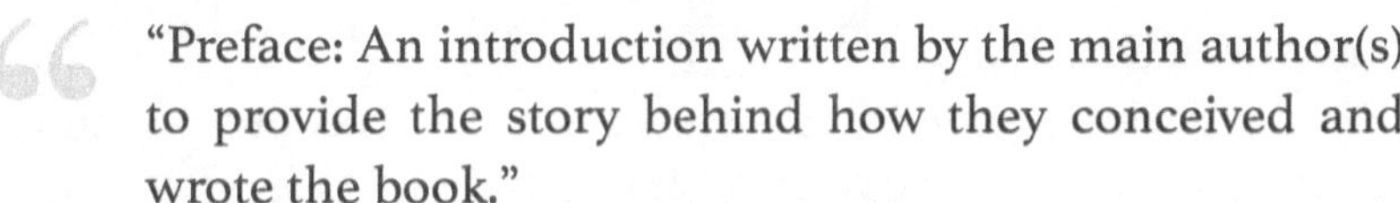

"Preface: An introduction written by the main author(s) to provide the story behind how they conceived and wrote the book."

— GETPROOFED.COM

I don't have to write this book.

You don't have to read this book.

There's not too much that "has to" in our worlds. On that note, let's get rid of what we have to do at least according to the most cliché of phrases:

"Our new Constitution is now established, everything seems to promise it will be durable; but, in this world, nothing is certain except death and taxes."

— BENJAMIN FRANKLIN

According to Mr. Franklin, it's only death and taxes. I'm going to go with that.

Everything else? It's your choice.

OK, OK, fine. I hear you. "I have to eat! I have to pay the rent! I have to go to school!"

My 17-year old says that last one on a regular basis. Yep, he has to go to school, according to the law.

Of course, if he chooses to break the law, ditch class, get in trouble, get expelled, etc., that's his choice.

You get the idea.

Maybe I should add here a bit about my intended audience.

You *usually* have a choice.

I wrote a book called "Decide: There's Usually a Choice. It's Usually Yours."

It's one of my favorite subtitles. I almost called that book "Choose" but that verb is maybe a bit too easy, almost fun-loving, and maybe some would see it as a luxury. Decide is a little tougher, more serious, more consequences.

It's telling that Decide is one of my favorite books but not necessarily one of my most popular. Why? Because it's not easy.

I have other books like Play and Pass the Sour Cream. I even have Secret Bus to Paradise. But Decide? That sounds difficult.

That's because it is.

 "Would you like the chocolate or vanilla gelato?"

That's a luxury. That's a choice.

However, the choice of ice cream doesn't keep you up at night (or at least I hope it doesn't).

But there's that nasty one that I know, for a fact, from experience, both mine and many others, does keep people up at night:

 "Should I write a book?"

The book you have in your hands (or maybe in your ears) is my 32nd book.

If I had a nickel for every person who came up to me and said some variation of:

 "I have a book idea!"

I could support my son's shoe addiction (OK, also a choice...).

I actually don't mind those people who come up to me and say they have a book idea. I believe we all have a book idea. I also believe we all have a book in us and, here we go, I'm going to say it right here, yep, in this book called "You Don't Have To," I do honestly believe that everyone *should* write a book. They also *could* write a book, in that they are capable of writing one.

But my follow-up is that you *don't have to*.

Do you see the difference?

- Should
- Could
- Have to

We haven't yet touched on what this book is really about.

Because of course it's not really about what you don't have to do—that would be a really short book (see note above about death and taxes).

It's about what you *want* to do.

And not just want to, but really, really, really want to do.

Back to the people who tell me they have a book idea.

"That's great," I usually say and leave it at that. This bland retort gets me one of three responses:

1. **Nothing:** we move on to the next topic. Often about the spinach dip.
2. **Surprise:** they were "expecting" more from me, Mr. Author of a Zillion Books, so they could continue to tell me about their book idea. But I don't continue, neither do they, and I leave it at that. Unless #3...

3. **Opening:** they sense that I just opened a door and they
   burst through and we talk books, ideas, tactics, strategies,
   and best of all: passion, perseverance, and patience.

#1 is over within seconds. #2 might hang around a minute or two. But #3? This is their opening to the portal to the universe of their future self.

I'm sure I'll talk more about basketball (and math and travel—some of my favorite topics) in this book but I want to tell a quick story about my basketball team to hammer home this point.

Here in The Netherlands, I'm the coach of the U16 (under 16-years-old) basketball team. In this country, sports aren't really big in schools but rather through organizations that are privately run.

In other words, it's not like you have to join a team. Sure, at school, they have gym class, which they have to do, but they don't have to join a sports team.

> **PRO TIP:** *I think sports teams are some of the best "educa-*
> *tion" we can get into our kids because they learn about*
> *teamwork, winning and losing with pride, and it gets*
> *them off the couch.*

We had a kid on the team last year who clearly didn't want to be there. But he "had to" according to his mom. In other words, he wasn't there by choice.

He hobbled through practice, he joked with players to the point where even they were annoyed that he was infringing on their own progress, and although he was usually upbeat, he counted the minutes until practice was over.

In the beginning, I did my best to motivate and inspire him. I involved him as much as I could, I got the team to support and encourage him, and for a while there, he seemed to like it and was getting better.

But still, it was clear he had to be there and didn't want to be there.

Another boy stayed after practice and asked me where he should aim his elbow when shooting a jump shot.

For a teacher or a coach, when the student asks questions, especially relevant ones, it's the dream come true. It's really all we hope for as teachers: that students want to learn, to improve, to be there.

I stayed after practice and we worked on his shot. He thanked me endlessly and practiced every chance he got. He got better. He couldn't wait for the games but even enjoyed practice.

I'm sure you can feel where I'm going here.

Boy #1 has to be there.

Boy #2 wants to be there.

Guess which one:

1. Will improve
2. Enjoys practice and the games
3. Is inspiring to his teammates
4. Becomes a team player
5. Gets even better because of #2 (enjoyment)

With my basketball example, it's so easy to see, isn't it?

Yet let's go back to writing a book (or meditating or intermittent fasting).

It's the same thing.

If you want the thing, if your passion for the thing is greater than your dislike (or annoyance or boredom or whatever) is for the thing, you can succeed.

Let's do a simple math equation.

Want the Thing > Don't Want the Other Thing

That symbol there is for greater than. So it reads wanting the thing has to be greater than not wanting the other thing.

Wanting to write a book is a greater force of energy or passion than not having written a book.

Wanting to meditate is greater than not wanting to doing it.

Wanting to intermittent fast is greater than not wanting to do it.

Remember when I said above I don't have to write this book? Part of me thinks this book is so simple and so basic that I don't have to write it because everyone knows this.

 Yeah, except uh, right, sure, that would be, um, me.

Do you know many years I spent **Not Doing the Thing** because that energy was greater than **Doing the Thing** because of fear or expectations or pressure or take-your-pick-of-reasons?

My fear for even starting the thing was greater than any whiff of ever possibly finishing or dare I even dream of succeeding with the thing.

During all those years, I had one thought in my head:

I *have to* write a book.

Sure, I wanted to write a book but it was more the feeling that I had to write the book that was holding me back.

Can you feel the difference?

That difference could have saved me nine years of my life (when I was hemming and hawing, back and forth, whining and moaning) and just not doing.

Can you feel the difference when we feel that we have to do a thing as compared to when that pressure is lifted and not only do we want to do the thing but it's more of an invitation, a gift, and we're allowed to do the thing.

That difference is what this book is about and why I'm writing it.

Repossible

While we're here, I'll just explain one more thing that's coming up. At the end of each chapter, I'll have these three bullet points. I'll put an explanation here and an example.

I use them to summarize the core of the message in the chapter.

It's also the name of my business, my brand, and the greater Repossible movement I founded and I'm a card-carrying member of.

- **Possible:** the easy way

- **Impossible:** the hard way
- **Repossible:** the way

Here's one of my favorite examples.

- **Possible:** tomorrow
- **Impossible:** yesterday
- **Repossible:** today

INTRODUCTION

As I keep referring people to this book, I keep wanting to change the title.

I find that this little book has a secret recipe, a Treasure Map towards more Clarity, Courage, and Confidence.

It's a 17-hour journey that has helped me so incredibly much, I wanted to get it more directly into the title.

So, if you're reading this, the title is probably:

17 Hours to to More Clarity, Courage, and Confidence (from 4 PM on Thursday to 9 AM on Friday)

With the subtitle:

A Repeatable Roadmap of Intermittent Fasting, Meditating, and Creating

I know, I'm a little crazy for wanting to change titles on my books (I do it rather often, actually) but they're like my darlings, my loves, my babies, and they grow up and evolve and ... well, at least I don't change the names of my kids as much as I do my books.

Enjoy 17 hours.

Bradley

ONE
ONE WORD (FOR ONE YEAR)

2024 Update !

 "I don't look to jump over 7-foot bars: I look around for 1-foot bars that I can step over."

— WARREN BUFFETT

One.

ONE-foot bar.

Just **ONE** bar to step over.

It's 2024. My latest challenge / program / book / course / retreat / workshop is called: ONE.

It's about focus. It's about Tiny Wins. It's about getting over the hurdles to make progress—so that we can make more progress.

It's about this:

- **ONE** word.
- In **ONE** day.
- For **ONE** year.

- For **ONE** person (you).
- In **ONE** book made up of **ONE** chapter.

It's been two years since I published the book you have in your hands. I keep changing the title because I keep wanting to "lower the bar" so that we can *get over more bars*.

I know it wasn't long ago back up at the beginning of this chapter but I'm going to repeat that quote here from Warren Buffett. The guy knows a few things about success.

 "I don't look to jump over 7-foot bars: I look around for 1-foot bars that I can step over."

— WARREN BUFFETT

I've had big programs and big books with big ideas.

But where I get the most joy is when people truly succeed, actually finish something, and smile with that grin that you only get when you've tried and won.

Won.

One.

Done.

Fun.

I'd like to invite you to check out the ONE challenge. It's about choosing ONE word for ONE year.

The thing is that I don't want you to write it on a napkin or "yeah, I'll think about it."

Nope.

I want to help you get something into your hands, something tangible, so this word is more real, more powerful, and it will help propel you through your year with more clarity, courage, and confidence.

If you'd like to get some clarity on you year (or DAY!) ahead, have a look at the book (One) and the program here:

go.repossible.com/17ONE

That link will give you a 25% discount on the online course or the in-person retreat.

Enjoy 17 Hours and when you'd like to get that ONE thing done, climb up that ONE rung of the ladder, come join us.

Repossible

- **Possible:** zero
- **Impossible:** infinity
- **Repossible:** one

PART I

CLARITY, COURAGE, AND CONFIDENCE

IT'S WHAT THIS BOOK HAS BECOME

"The clarity to know what to do, the courage to do it, and the confidence to finish."

— BRADLEY CHARBONNEAU

1

———

WHAT THIS BOOK IS OFFERING

PLAIN, SIMPLE, AND 17 HOURS

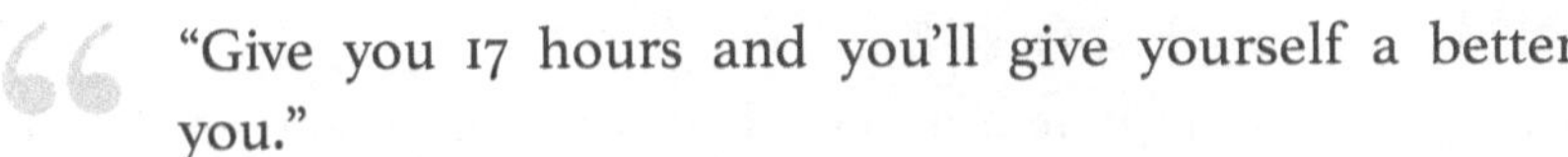

"Give you 17 hours and you'll give yourself a better you."

> — BRADLEY CHARBONNEAU (TWEAKED FROM A
> CAR INSURANCE COMMERCIAL WITH A GECKO)

This book has been a work in progress for more than a year. The good news and the bad news is that it just keeps getting better.

That's bad news because I keep adding to it.

That's good news because you're going to get the best of it.

17 Hours to Clarity, Courage, and Confidence

I want to get the main message of this book across quickly here before you get bogged down in oddball chapters with titles such as *Smile and Wave, Boys, Smile and Wave.*

Elsewhere I've shared how this book started (as a joke) but now it's morphed into something that I can't emphasize enough the importance of.

I'm usually a pretty modest guy but I'm going to be un-modest for a moment.

You'll see I like bullet lists. Here goes.

1. I have written 32 books (and feel like I'm just getting started)
2. I moved my family from the US to The Netherlands
3. I closed down my business to pursue my dream (of being a writer)
4. I've been to Hel (and back)
5. I wrote and published every single day without missing a single one for 2,808 days in a row
6. I have the energy of a 28-year old
7. I have the wisdom of an 82-year old

OK, back to my modest self.

I write this not to brag but to explain why I have searched for an answer to the question:

 "Bradley, how do you do it?"

The thing was that I didn't know how I did it. I also didn't realize I was "doing" anything. I was just doing.

I didn't have a strategy or a plan or a roadmap.

I just did. Created things. Finished stuff.

The Treasure Map

I'll go into this in more detail in the chapter brilliantly titled Treasure Map, but here is the map in a nutshell.

There are just three steps. Don't look away, you might miss them.

These three things, when done in this order, over a period of 17 hours, is my secret to *clarity*, *courage*, and *confidence*.

1. Fast

2. Meditate
3. Create

That's it. Those three things. Ideally in that order.

I'll even spill the goods right here and now (and get into more detail later) for those of you wondering what this book is all about and want to know right now before you read further.

> *Stop eating at 4 PM. Go to bed 2 hours earlier than usual.*
> *Wake up 2 hours earlier than usual. Meditate. Create.*
> *Record. Finish by 9 AM.*

That's 17 hours.
Remember the title of this part of the book:

Clarity. Courage. Confidence.

17 hours to get more of each (or all) of those.
That's what this book is about.

- **Possible:** read, ponder, wonder, maybe do
- **Impossible:** get from the reading of this book the same results as the doing what we're suggesting
- **Repossible:** let it sink in that it's only 17 hours

P.S. I was listening to one of my favorite creators recently and he asked if we noticed that there were no weight loss programs that offered, "Lose 10 pounds in 10 years." Along the same lines, I actually don't recommend writing every single day for 2,808 days—or at least not making that huge number the goal. It starts with the first step. Sure, 17 days, 17 weeks, 17 months will be awesome possum. But it starts with your first 17 hours.

BONUS CONTENT
WRITER, SPEAKER, NARRATOR

 "It's never crowded along the extra mile."

— WAYNE DYER

I used to be content with writing books. Words on pages like the ones you're reading now.

But it evolved. I evolved.

For example, I'm a huge fan of listening to audiobooks but an even bigger fanatic of narrating my audiobooks.

I've also been recording videos every single week since January 1, 2020 (and I upload them). You can subscribe to my YouTube Channel (go.repossible.com/youtube) or I'll email you every Thursday with the video (tt.repossible.com).

So I can't seem to "just write books" any longer. I want to have videos and audio and links and comments and discussions.

Therefore, in recent books I've been creating Bonus Content. The bonus content for this book is free and you can access it here: go.repossible.com/ydht-bonus.

- **Possible:** checking out the bonus content later
- **Impossible:** understand that there is bonus content, think about going to check it out, not doing it, and getting the same benefit as having gone
- **Repossible:** check out the bonus content now

PART II

NO, REALLY. YOU DON'T.

"Freedom is what you do with what's been done to you."

— JEAN-PAUL SARTRE

3

PLEASE READ THE PREFACE

OF COURSE … YOU DON'T HAVE TO

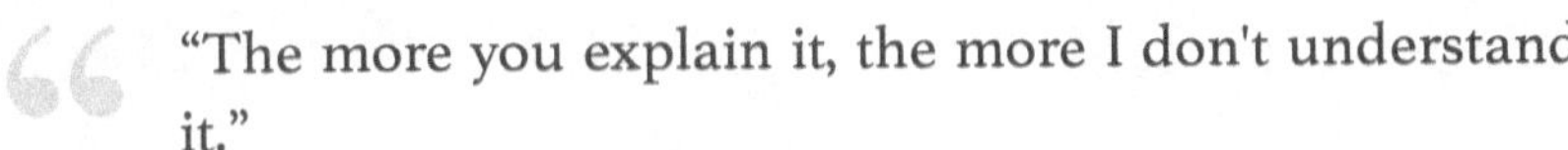 "The more you explain it, the more I don't understand it."

— MARK TWAIN

There are some e-readers that will open up your book right to chapter one.

I get it, it makes sense. That's where books often start. Especially fiction books.

But many (most?) of my books are as much about the meta content as they are about the content. The why I'm writing the books is sometimes even more important than the message of the book itself.

If you don't read the preface, you might not get where I'm going with this book.

Especially with my addiction to witty titles that don't always mean something to everyone, I often need to explain my book in a section like the preface.

- **Possible:** keep reading
- **Impossible:** keep reading and pretend you read the preface
- **Repossible:** read the preface

4

OOPS, I DID IT AGAIN

CREATING BREEDS MORE CREATING

> "The process of writing is like creating a game of dominoes: The first domino creates the second incident, and so forth until the end."
>
> — ASGHAR FARHADI

This book became bigger than I originally thought it was going to be.

It was originally just a play on a book called "You Must Write a Book" when I was running a program to help people write their book. The program was called "How to Write Your Worst Book Ever." It was great fun. We had some big breakthroughs.

But as I worked on this book and talked about the title with others, I realized there were other things that we "didn't have to do" and yet thought we did or should.

The main ones together were these (and in this order):

1. Fasting
2. Meditating
3. Creating

Those three things have become a "formula" or a system for me to achieve fantastical levels of clarity, courage, and confidence.

It seems so simple. It is so simple.

It's not always easy but it's simple.

As I wrote, it became more and more apparent that this little trio of actions, when put together, was even more powerful than their individual elements separately.

That's when this book became more than I thought it was in the beginning.

What started out as a bit of a joke became something useful and even important and finally it morphed into a system, a reliable routine that you can do, over the course of just 17 hours, and start to build that clarity, courage, and confidence that I have experienced.

One of my personal favorite books I wrote and one of my most popular is called Create. It's about taking action. Fearless (or even full of fear but doing it anyway), tiny, regular action.

This book started as a joke and dare I say I think it's become one of my favorite books and possibly one of my most helpful.

Because I dared to take action on an idea.

Thanks for being here, thanks for reading.

Let's get rolling.

- **Possible:** jog around the block
- **Impossible:** finish the marathon (without taking the first step)
- **Repossible:** take the first step

5

PRIORITY #1

NOT THE ONLY PRIORITY, NOT FOREVER, BUT FOR NOW, NUMBER ONE

> "The key is not to prioritize what's on your schedule, but to schedule your priorities."
>
> — STEPHEN COVEY

I'm in a hotel lobby pretty early on a Sunday morning. I woke up even earlier, did my meditation, and I know my wife will sleep hours more.

Here are some things I could do right now:

1. Stay in bed and sleep (for me, when I'm awake, I'm awake)
2. Listen to something in my headphones
3. Stare at the ceiling
4. Read my book
5. Get dressed and go for a walk in the city we're in (Groningen FYI)

I'm pretty sure yesterday was the beginning of the Final Four (college basketball tournament in the U.S.). I'd really like to watch that.

In fact, as I type, I have just made a deal with myself that I can watch it after this chapter (and the one called "Hey, It Didn't Work.").

Priority #1

I think it was the film "Good Morning, Vietnam" where a young Vietnamese boy had the Mercedes medallion from the American guy's car and said something like, "Mercedes Number One!"

> *It very well could have been another movie entirely and that something else was Number One but go with me here for a minute.*

> *Speaking of distractions, as is the topic of this chapter, I could go right now and spend valuable, creative, early morning time trying to find that scene and get it just right but I can almost guarantee you I would lose my train of thought ... in fact, I am losing it as I type these words so I'll get back to it now.*

I have this image of the Vietnamese boy holding up his index finger and very enthusiastically smiling and saying repeatedly to the guy "Number One!"

This chapter right here is my Priority Number One this morning. My Priority Number Two is the chapter, "Hey, It Didn't Work." Number three is the Final Four.

If you know me a bit and know that, for example, I wrote consecutively for 2,808 days without missing a day (and wrote 31 books in the process), you might think that such frivolous things as a tiny hierarchy on a Sunday morning would be easy for me but I can guarantee you, it's not.

I am laughing quietly to myself as I write this as I feel like the little boy who is eating his broccoli only because he knows he'll get dessert and if he doesn't eat his broccoli he won't get dessert at all today.

The dilemma here is that I'm both the little boy and his mother at the same time! I have the broccoli (this chapter) and the dessert (watching the Final Four recap on YouTube) in my control.

Be The Mom

Do what you have to do but make this a priority.

Remember, we're not saying it has to be Priority #1 for every single day for the rest of your life and you can never have dessert on any day if you don't do it.

Be the mom. Be the one who knows how important the broccoli is and get it done. First.

And also be the child. With the power of that broccoli, your day will bounce ahead, rocket forward, and blossom outwards.

TriTiTo

While in the woods last year, I somehow had this Amazonian tribal moment (no offense to the REAL Amazonia tribes) and came up with this mantra: TriTiTo (tree / tie / toe).

- Trigger
- Time
- Together

I add this here if you're struggling being both the kid and the mom and are looking for ways to make this chapter (this thing you're trying to do, be it fasting, meditation, or creating) your number one priority.

Trigger Time Together came about from *group projects* that had a *clear goal* to be accomplished in a *specified time frame*.

So rather than saying, "OK, fast, meditate, and create every so often for the rest of your life alone." (Ouch, even writing that sounds cruel!), instead saying something like:

> "Let's 10 of us do a fasting, meditating, and creating long weekend retreat starting Thursday and wrapping up Sunday afternoon."

Even better would be to add a bit of a concrete, measurable goal to the Sunday afternoon. For example, if writing is your goal, to have written three chapters (one per day).

- **Trigger:** set up the group, initiate inspiration
- **Time:** a fixed schedule with a start time and a deadline (and stick to it)
- **Together:** it's easier, more powerful and just plain more fun to do this in a (small) group

Oops, I Did It Again

I can't guarantee this will always happen but here I am, way down further in this chapter and I'm into it, loving it, feeling good. I've even almost forgotten about the basketball game.

Or rather, I haven't forgotten about the basketball game but I know this is the order, the sequential order in which I will both finish and succeed this morning.

I hope I can convey the power of this here.

By making the writing (or the fasting or the meditating or the _______ whatever it is you want to get done) the priority for the morning or for the session, by starting, persevering, and finishing, we build muscle, we create a sense of accomplishment and, honest and truly, the rest of our day will go better than had we done it the other way around.

This Is Hard

You might think this is easy for me. I still want to watch the game. I will watch the game. I was struggling the first few paragraphs and wanted to give up, to make an excuse, to say to myself:

> "Oh, I'm not in the mood right now and this chapter isn't going to be that great anyway, I should just watch the game and write this chapter this afternoon. Yeah, that will be fine. I mean, right? It will, right? Hello? Anyone? Bueller?"

I won't win an award for writing this chapter first this morning. As I look around the lobby, no one will know if I'm writing a chapter of a book or if I'm watching North Carolina versus Duke.

Only one person will know and only one person will care.

Me.

Well, maybe two.

You.

Me and you.

Me because my day will be better thanks to doing this first.

You because I got this chapter done and you're reading it and hopefully the power of the message will sink in for you.

An author in the "How to Write Your Easiest Book Ever" (which is going on right now and is yet another piece of motivation (TriTiTo) for me to write this chapter) said something like:

> "If the message of my book helps one single person, it's a success. In fact, if that one single person is me, it's a success. If it then goes on to help one more person (and then another), it's all icing on the cake."

No one will know if I finish this chapter. I look around the café here and no one knows what I'm doing or if I'm going to finish.

But I know.

I know if I'm done for the morning.

And with that, I'm done. Priority Number One has been accomplished and the day has barely begun.

I like mantras so here's one we could say, quietly in our minds, or maybe whisper quietly in this hotel café lobby:

 "Finishing my tiny priority #1 task this morning will give me confidence, boost my energy, and make my day better."

We don't need to share our accomplishments on social media or scream them from the rooftops (although you're welcome to). The only person who needs to know you made a choice this morning, you prioritized and you got your task done, is you.

We are often our harshest critics.

Give yourself a small win early in the day and let it domino forward throughout your day.

- **Possible:** be only the child
- **Impossible:** be only the mom
- **Repossible:** be the child, be the mom, eat your broccoli first and cherish your dessert

6

———

FEELING A LITTLE DOWN
NOT ANYMORE

> "I was lucky enough when it came to sports and work ethic to be taught some basics that continue to be important."

— JOE NAMATH

I don't know what was up. Last night, I was just feeling rather down. I'm struggling to get people into the Easiest Book Ever challenge, my audiobook sales are down, and Luca got a bad grade on his geography test.

PRO TIP: See the chapter called 5:55 for how I solved this.

So last night, I skipped dinner, went to bed early, woke up early, meditated and wrote.

I feel like a different person than I did last night.

Last night, I was thinking:

> "Maybe I should just get a job."

— ME, LAST NIGHT

Now I'm on top of the world.

I also know "on top of the world" is where I enjoy being. I mean, duh, doesn't everyone?

I'm not so sure.

What is your default energy level? Or as Esther Hicks calls it, your flying disc. Are you on a low-flying disc or a high-flying disc?

Last night, I was on a low-flying disc.

This morning, I'm back on my high-flying disc.

How can I keep that up?

Stick to what I know works. Stick to the plan, the roadmap, the treasure map:

1. Fast
2. Meditate
3. Create

I'm writing this chapter to myself so I know what to do when I'm feeling down, when I'm flying low.

I know I don't have to do it (ha, see how I'm using the game of the book title even on myself!?), but I know the benefits of doing it.

Which is going to win?

Keep going with the low-flying disc and trying new things all the time?

Or get back on the high-flying disc and going with what you know works for you.

Oh, and if you don't yet know it works for you, have you given it a genuine effort?

I just wrote another chapter of this book (this chapter here) and I also feel better.

Create.

- **Possible:** push harder
- **Impossible:** try new stuff always
- **Repossible:** go back to the basics

7

THAT'S STUPID

THAT'S GREAT THAT IT WORKS FOR YOU BUT IT'S NOT FOR ME

"If you have learned how to disagree without being disagreeable, then you have discovered the secret of getting along - whether it be business, family relations, or life itself."

— BERNARD MELTZER

I'm going to make this chapter short and hard hitting and just get to the point.

If someone thinks your idea is "stupid" or "That's great that it works for you but it's not for me." it's highly possible that you just have the wrong audience.

Let's revisit my favorite examples:

- The high-school boys in biology class
- The 14-year-old kid who is in basketball because his mother wants him to play a sport
- A yoga enthusiast who doesn't want to meditate because yoga is her thing

There are varying degrees of pushback here. From the quiet basketball kid who would just rather sit on the sidelines to the snickering students in biology to the, I kid you not, yoga fan who tells you again and again and more and more forcefully, that she doesn't want to meditate and she just wants to stick with yoga—and thinks you should do yoga, too.

> ***PRO TIP:*** *I bet it sounds like that yoga person should just be left alone. That's EXACTLY what needs to happen. The biology kids MUST be there. The basketball kid not so much. But yoga sorceress? Just leave her in her dog's pose.*

Remember, this book was mostly written because I heard myself saying (maybe way too often ...) that people didn't "have to do" the thing I was talking about.

It usually came about when I was explaining something about any of the three main elements of this book, fasting, meditating, or creating, and the person I was talking to would get defensive of their position of not wanting to do the thing.

But then they would ask me again questions such as:

> "So, tell me honestly, Bradley, how do you manage to wake up early, have such energy, and crank out books, videos, and podcasts, interviews and courses, and keep going after years and still have such a positive attitude and even form groups and workshops and ... "

> — THEY

If I then mentioned fasting, meditation or creating they would push those ideas away as if those weren't my real answers and they wanted the "real" answers but I was holding those back.

Simple But Not Easy

More often than not, people don't believe you if the answer is too simple or easy.

My answers were simple: **do one or all of these three things.**

The implementation is not easy: actually doing these things with integrity.

 "That's Stupid"

— THEY

There were times when I felt like a used car salesman and that I was pushing these things onto people. In a way, of course, I was. They asked how I succeeded in certain things and I told them.

But when they didn't like the answers or wanted different answers, often their response would be, either in these words or in so many words, "That's Stupid."

That's when it's time to head back to the all-you-can-eat buffet and get another dumpling.

That's both simple and easy.

And not stupid.

Well, unless you really don't like dumplings at which point you might say, "That's stupid."

See how it's a vicious circle?

Then it's truly time to Smile and Wave.

- **Possible:** keep trying
- **Impossible:** sell harder—and succeed
- **Repossible:** smile and wave

8

SMILE AND WAVE, BOYS, SMILE AND WAVE

KEEP YOUR COOL

 "Smile and wave, boys, smile and wave."

— THE PENGUINS FROM MADAGASCAR

This chapter is for those of us with an idea that others don't want.

In the previous chapter, That's Stupid, we talked about those people who really just don't want to hear it.

They might want to get the result you're talking about but they're not interested in the roadmap (or system or step) to get there.

Or at least not *your* roadmap.

I haven't seen the film for years but those penguins are still a hit. They even have their own spinoff movie.

They can be a deceiving, conniving, sneaky bunch and there are several scenes in which they say their famous line. Usually, they're hiding something. For example, they're in the zoo and there's a big bucket of fish behind them and they don't want to attract attention to it (so they can then eat it all).

In a way, this is similar.

Although I take offense to calling myself and what I'm doing "deceiving, conniving or sneaky!"

But in a way, that's what others sometimes think I'm doing.

Remember, I'm an author. I'm a speaker, teacher, course creator, coach, and presenter.

I'm up on stage or narrating words into microphones and I don't even pretend that I'm not preaching something or teaching or sharing information or experiences. That's exactly what I do.

> **PRO TIP:** *It's funny how creating works. Here I am writing this chapter about the penguins. I had a tiny idea to begin with but here I am 268 words into the chapter and I see that it's even more relevant than I had imagined. Please take this into consideration when you're debating whether or not you could or should create something today. You never know where it's going to go and it could explode into an awesome chapter. Or, sure, it could also dud out and fizzle into the nothingness. A risk every single time I put fingers to the keyboard or hit record. A risk I'm willing to take 100% of the time.*

Where were we?

Oh yes, deceiving, conniving or sneaky.

I honestly believe that some people honestly believe that I'm trying to trick them.

Sort of a side note ... do you know much about vitamin D? If you read a bit about it, it's a bit of a wonder vitamin. In fact, if you read a bit more, you might learn it's not even a vitamin. However, do you see ads for vitamin D? No. Why not?

Simple. There's no money in it.

Water. There's another. I have an entire chapter on it. Am I trying to sell you fancy water? No. Tap is fine. It's a freaking wonder element.

I've been wanting to make a YouTube sketch (very SNL) about the team planning the catering for the Intermittent Fasting Conference.

I laugh just imagining the scene:

> *"So Jill, do you have the welcome drink covered?"*
> *"Got it, Fernando. Water glasses will be half full."*
> *"Awesome. Slim Jim, you have the hors d'oeuvres ready?"*
> *"But Fernando ... "*
> *"Just kidding, Jim, I know there aren't any hors d'oeuvres!*
>   *Jill, what about dessert?"*
> *"Uh ... "*
> *"Kidding! Gotcha!"*

I know, I have my own sense of humor. If you'd like to hire my "Intermittent Fasting Catering Company" for your next event, just go to emptyplates.com.

Are you feeling how I'm feeling like the penguins yet?

Here I am in a book suggesting you:

1. Don't eat anything
2. Meditate alone
3. Create something

What could I sell? A pen?

OK, now I'm really feeling the conniving penguin. Of course I could make all of this easier for you—and that IS my dream.

Here, I'll share.

I'd love to have a 5-day workshop where we don't eat much, we wake up early and meditate, and then we create stuff.

So what am I "selling"?

TriTiTo

This comes from my "How to Write Your Easiest Book Ever" program which stands for:

- Trigger
- Time
- Together

There's an action or **Trigger** (a workshop) and reaction (your accepting the invitation) and a specific **Time** (5 days, starting e.g. April 1) and it's not alone but **Together** with others.

You could do it all on your own (well, except for that last part) at no cost. Not only at no cost but you'd be saving money by buying less food!

In a way, I'm a terrible businessman. I should be selling vitamin supplements, guided meditation audio, and courses on how to write books easily.

Ha, OK, that last one is a joke because I DO offer a program on how to write books easily.

> *Dear Reader,*
> *This chapter is getting out of hand. But I have to say, I'm*
> *loving it. This is Creation in Action. Yet on the one*
> *hand, I'm stating how innocent I am (by suggesting you*
> *don't need to buy "no food" from me) yet in fact I do*
> *have a writing program so I'm not completely "inno-*
> *cent" like the penguins. But the penguins usually aren't*
> *innocent either. See how I'm digging a hole for myself*
> *here? Yet I'm owning up to it, I'm being transparent, I'm*
> *stating it as I see it and I also believe in what I'm doing*
> *—unlike those sneaking penguins!*
> *The Author*

This chapter started out for those of us, like myself, who want to help others.

That's it. Plain and simple.

Yet those others are not always understanding or willing or grateful or anything but annoyed that we're trying to get them to do something they don't want to do in the way we are suggesting and the way they don't want to do it.

To them, I say plainly, and thus this book: You Don't Have To.

You know how those marketing companies offer scripts to use for your sales calls? Here's the script for those who think what you're doing is stupid.

1. Person asks you how you've succeeded.
2. You tell them.
3. They ask for more detail. (**PRO TIP:** this could mean they don't understand your process even if it's super simple or more probably they don't believe it could be so easy and/or simple to solve the problem you have solved but they haven't.)
4. You provide more detail.
5. They prod for a different answer.
6. You say you only have the one answer.
7. They want a different answer.
8. You don't have one.
9. You smile.
10. You say, "You Don't Have To."
11. To which they have no response.
12. To which you add the wave to your smile.

Smile and wave, boys, smile and wave.

- **Possible:** smile and say nothing
- **Impossible:** wave it all away
- **Repossible:** be the penguin

PART III

BUT IF YOU REALLY, REALLY, REALLY WANT TO...

"Work consists of whatever a body is obliged to do. Play consists of whatever a body is not obliged to do."

— MARK TWAIN

9
———

A CLEAR PATH FORWARD
CREATE YOUR OWN RITUAL

> "Your vision will become clear only when you can look into your own heart. Who looks outside, dreams; who looks inside, awakes."

— CARL JUNG

I'm a tinkerer, a creator, a mad scientist if you will. I like playing, creating, and usually my goal, even my success is to "See what happens."

That's when I'm happiest. When I don't need the outcome, don't expect it, and there's not even really a goal.

Yet here we are. Together. Well, sort of. I'm writing this book and you're reading it.

Sure, I could say:

> "Wing it! Give it all a try! See what happens!"

I've tried that. It doesn't usually go well. Because I also think back to when I was starting with all of this and that's what I did. It took forever. There was more failure than success, more setbacks than progress, more backward than forward.

Which is why it's a good thing I didn't write this book then.

Because now I have a system. For you. If you don't resonate with the word *system*, let's try on some others for size.

1. Approach
2. Blueprint
3. Framework
4. Method
5. Model
6. Paradigm
7. Plan
8. Practice
9. Process
10. Roadmap
11. Routine
12. Ritual
13. Strategy
14. Structure
15. System
16. Technique
17. Treasure Map

Wow, I didn't think I'd get that many. 17 ways I didn't used to do things.

> **BEHIND THE SCENES:** *I must admit here that I have never been one for all of this structure. I can't say that I will always use one. It's more fun without one. But if you're going to go from A to B, it will help. It will help get you there faster, more easily, and you can then repeat it and improve. I'm half stating this here so that I hear it myself ... ;-)*

It's not that I thought I had a better roadmap. In fact, I honestly usually didn't have any roadmap at all.

How does that work? Well, slowly.

I want to provide you, in this book, with a simple roadmap, a clear path forward to save you the time and hassle and frustration in coming up with a plan towards more clarity, courage, and confidence, in the direction of action, a step closer to whatever goal you're after.

There is absolutely wiggle room in this plan laid out here for alterations, improvements, and new and unknown elements. Go for it, change it, do whatever you want with it.

But first, if I dare be so bold as to suggest, master first these simple three steps and then start tweaking.

Either I'm a brilliant mind or people just try to obfuscate the simplicity of the reality.

I heard a quote the other day that I can't remember exactly but it was something like:

"The amateur has a strategy, the professional has a process."

— SOMEONE SAID SOMETHING LIKE THIS

Have you ever noticed that monks and gurus (well, the truly great ones) are often pretty funny? They're light, sometimes silly, and they admit that what they're teaching is both simple and easy. But, of course, many things are simple and easy once you've been doing them for a long time.

Which is exactly my point.

I smile as I type this because I see the steps laid out in this book as simple and easy. I will repeat them again and again. In fact, I'll do it right now just so you know I'm not hiding anything (or at least I'm not intentionally hiding anything!).

Let's see if I can get the three steps as simple and concise as possible.

1. **Fast:** stop eating at 4 PM; go to sleep 2 hours earlier than usual
2. **Meditate:** wake up 2 hours earlier than usual; meditate for 20 to 40 minutes
3. **Create:** write or record (audio or video) whatever comes to you

Ha, I did it! This book into three simple lines.

You know what's weird? (Can you tell I'm in a playful mood this morning as I type this? I hope you feel the connection with me that I feel with you, the reader, as I type this.) What's weird is that if I were some über guru on some morning news show or being interviewed by some famous person and we had fancy graphics and testimonials from Hollywood actors (apparently, that makes whatever you're doing more believable … ;-)) and a million people had done this and they all had life-altering mystical experiences where they visited planet Pluto (or maybe visited the dog Pluto from Disney!) and then—and only then—would you "believe" that it worked.

Well, I shouldn't say it's weird. It's true. It's what works. When lots and lots of people do a thing and have success and then it's spread to even more people with more success then—and only then—is it a success.

I dare to disagree.

Well, not disagree as much as want to offer an alternative.

I'm just a guy. I'm sitting here on my couch on a Sunday morning writing this with Pepper, my dog, next to me as my trusted advisor, and he knows it works.

How does he know it works?

Because, and this is going to be really weird especially if you thought that last bit wasn't that weird: my goal is to have a mindset more like him.

He's repeatedly full of pure joy, bliss even, on a daily if not hourly basis.

An important takeaway from Pepper: it's not that he's in 24/7 bliss.

He has it, then it subsides and he'll have it again later. He's not expecting it, he doesn't feel down or bad or like he's missing out when he's not feeling it. He just is. When it's time for joy, he's all in.

If I were to stand up right now, put on my shoes and take him into the woods (which I'll do when I'm done with this chapter), he'll be, literally, jumping for joy.

Yet we do the same thing every single day.

And he jumps for joy every single day.

Literally. Jumping. For. Joy.

Every. Single. Day.

We have a clear path for success. I put on my shoes, he knows we're going into the woods, he's joyful.

Remember the gurus and simple and easy?

With Pepper, it's simple and easy.

With what I'm proposing in this book, it's a clear path forward and, in my humble opinion, it's simple and easy.

Fast, meditate, create.

One, two, three.

Put on the shoes and go to the woods.

Last night we went to a Greek restaurant and had gyros and I had a few beers. I wasn't following the plan. This morning I don't feel as good. Which is also the beauty of the *fast* and *meditate* and *create* methodology: you don't have to do it. You don't have to do it every day. You can do it when you want to feel better.

I often quote a dentist who, when asked "Which teeth should I brush?" replied "Only the ones you want to keep."

It's the same thing here. Only fast and meditate and create on days you want to feel better, see more clearly, move forward.

What's the title of this book?

You Don't Have To.

You don't have to do this. You don't have to do any of it. You can choose to do some of it, one element, two elements, or all three. You don't have to do it but if you want to do it, you can follow these simple steps.

There's usually a choice.
It's usually yours.

- **Possible:** no path
- **Impossible:** one and only one path
- **Repossible:** your path

10

TREASURE MAP

CREATE A RITUAL FOR YOURSELF TO FIND TREASURE EACH TIME

> "To be satisfied with a little, is the greatest wisdom; and he that increaseth his riches, increaseth his cares; but a contented mind is a hidden treasure, and trouble findeth it not."
>
> — AKHENATON

We can follow the path. It might be straight. Hopefully not. But let's practice getting from A to B so that we can then get to C.

From C, we'll see what else is around.

Looking for a Roadmap? How about a Treasure Map?

Roadmaps are terrific for getting from Point A to Point B.

The thing with meditation and creating is that although you think you're heading towards Point B and you might end up there, often the most interesting (and beneficial and fun) can be a different destination.

Meditation and creation are not math. It's not 1 + 1 = 2. It's more

like quantum physics where there are jumps and equations that seem
to defy reality (see the chapter titled "Dawn" for example).

A Treasure Map

Below is a possible map, call it a roadmap if you like, but I prefer treasure map as there are possible jewels all along the way.

At first, follow it as best you can but once your confidence builds,
stray from the path and let the explorer in you discover the unknown.

1. 4 PM: have your last meal of the day, ideally not too heavy;
   water, too.
2. Evening: keep up the water intake. Don't overdo it but
   drink more than you usually do (which is probably not
   enough!).
3. Go to bed early. 2 hours earlier than normal.
4. Don't look at screens in bed (although an e-reader is OK).
   Ideally, listen to soft music and lull yourself into a
   meditative slumber.
5. "Plan" your dreams and/or meditation.
6. Wake up early (see point #2 ;-)). Maybe 2 hours earlier
   than normal (did you also go to sleep 2 hours earlier than
   normal?).
7. Use the bathroom, have a glass (or 2) of water but don't do
   other stuff (e.g. clean up, wash dishes, turn on any screens,
   check email, etc.).
8. Set up your ritual for meditation.
9. Sit down.
10. Take a deep breath. Or several.
11. Reward yourself, congratulate yourself for having skipped
    dinner, drunk lots of water, gone to bed early, and woken
    up early.
12. Dig into your meditation.
13. Enjoy.
14. Immediately afterwards, write (or record) your findings.

15. Save that recording.
16. Start your day by 9 AM
17. Smile.

The best part in my humble opinion is that you don't know what you're going to find. It's not like jogging where every single day is the same path and the same kilometers and you pass the same park or house and you know it all by heart.

Sure, the steps are here, the path is similar but it's the magical and the mystical and the unknown that make all of this worthwhile. That's the treasure. The unknown.

If the treasure at the end of the map were always the same, I'm pretty sure I would have stopped meditating (and maybe fasting and creating) years ago.

Yet it stays different. In fact, **it's exactly that difference that keeps me going and wanting more and to get better at it, more efficient at it.**

The word Treasure Map is light and fun and brings along images of pirates and deserted islands and palm trees and glittery treasure.

What might your treasure be?

That's the beauty: I won't know. I can't know.

In fact, you might not know. Until you take action.

My true wish for you is not to go just from A to B to C. It's to go from A to B to See.

- **Possible:** no map
- **Impossible:** one map
- **Repossible:** treasure map

11

HEY, IT DIDN'T WORK

IT'S NOT PERFECTION, IT'S A PRACTICE

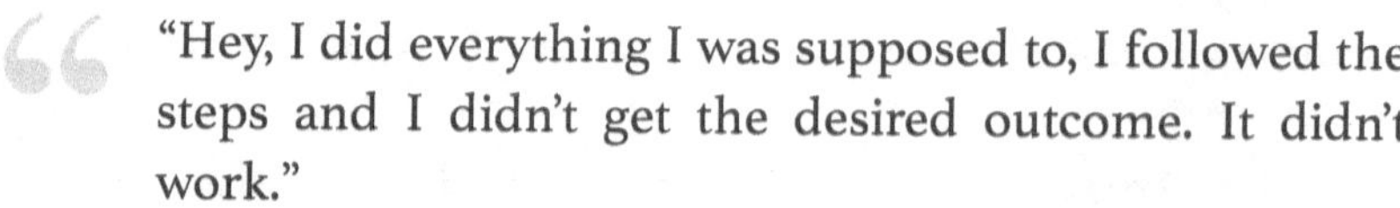

> "Hey, I did everything I was supposed to, I followed the steps and I didn't get the desired outcome. It didn't work."

— MAYBE YOU

I can imagine the thought because I, too, of course, have said such things after trying something that was "supposed to" work.

Here I am as the author of this book and I'm laying out a system, a plan, a roadmap, even a Treasure Map as I like to call it, that could lead to a desired outcome.

I'm suggesting:

1. **Fast:** intermittent fast, or don't eat for a number of hours
2. **Meditate:** wake up and do a meditation
3. **Create:** post meditation, create something (write, record, etc.)

I'm suggesting it might have outcomes like this:

1. Declutter your mind, let the good and big ideas land, etc. (**Clarity**), but also lose weight, sleep better, sleep more efficiently, etc.
2. Make, build, do and dare start something (turn nothing into something), etc. (**Courage**)
3. Finish, celebrate, and take pride in what you finish. (**Confidence**)

But if you do the three things and you don't get the clarity of mind or the chapter written, I can absolutely understand you wanting to say, "Hey, it didn't work."

- Of the three events, **fasting** is the simplest. Don't eat. That's it.
- **Meditation** is a wild card. Who knows what's going to happen!
- **Creating** is similarly open ended and toying with the unknown.

Although I can by no means guarantee any of the steps separately will do anything in the short list above or even that, when combined and done sequentially over a period of 17 hours, this will grant any or some or all of the desired outcomes, I can say this: it's a practice, not a perfection.

Like brushing teeth, jogging around the block, or anything we do on a regular basis for the greater good of the whole, **we might not notice when it "works."**

Yep, we might hope we lose some weight or even just "feel lighter" on the first morning. Sure, we hope that during the meditation we'll have mystical, out-of-body experiences or that when we put pen to paper or fingers to keyboard, we'll fly along and create our master-works, but more often than not, it's probably going to be incremental changes, possibly barely noticeable improvements.

But what's that concept that we become just 1% better each day? After a year, we're 365% better, right? What might that look like?

Or after seven days or seven sessions (fasting, meditating, creating), what might happen?

So if it doesn't "happen" on the first try or then it does happen again and again but then it doesn't happen, know that it's part of the game, the puzzle, the mystery and playing it is our role, our task, and when we see it as a game and playing the game, being a participant in the game is more important than winning the game, then and only then can we say, quietly, whispering to ourselves:

 "Hey, it worked."

Smile as you say it. Because now you know, even when you think it didn't work, it worked.

- **Possible:** it works sometimes (complete with fireworks)
- **Impossible:** it works every single time (complete with fireworks)
- **Repossible:** it works

12

LIVE (A LITTLE) OF YOUR FUTURE DREAM LIFE NOW

EVEN IF YOU THINK YOU'RE NOT READY

> "Your entire life only happens in this moment. The present moment is life itself. Yet, people live as if the opposite were true and treat the present moment as a stepping stone to the next moment - a means to an end."
>
> — ECKHART TOLLE

We're in Athens, Greece as I type this (on my ancient laptop ... OK, maybe *ancient* in this city isn't quite the right word!).

I am as "guilty" as most of us who can quickly be less satisfied with the present because it's not quite what I had envisioned it to be (in the past).

Did you catch that?

In the past, I envisioned a future and yet, just like the word tomorrow, it never is here. The future, by definition, doesn't exist. It's always tomorrow, it's always ahead of us, we will never catch it.

So what do we have left?

The present.

I had envisioned a life where I could be traveling in a faraway place, waking up early and creating, probably writing, and publishing books *like there was no tomorrow* (ha, funny guy, right?), and, oh, I don't know, going on a bike tour of the city with my family and ending up in a colorful bar later that same night and stirring up raucous conversations with strangers.

Oops.

That's exactly what happened yesterday.

One of my favorite books is titled "Secret Bus to Paradise." I wrote it many years back now but I mention it because even back then I was *living* my dream and not only *dreaming* about it.

It wasn't a bus to a paradise that we see in the magazines or on Instagram. I made my own private paradise. It's a great little story I can highly recommend. Ha, I'm laughing a little bit to myself here as I'm recommending one of my own books.

But there you have it. That is part of my dream: I have books I have written already that are good and I recommend them inside of other books.

How did that happen?

Because I didn't wait to write the perfect book (well, I did spend about nine years not writing ...) but I finally started writing on November 1, 2012, and kept going. Some books aren't great, some are good, and some are brilliant. Seriously, yep, I'm saying that about my own work.

Yet had I waited to only write that one perfect book, it most likely never would have appeared because I'd be so caught up in hoping, trying, and fiddling to make it perfect (whatever perfect means ...) that it wouldn't be in your hands, it would be in a drawer and I'd probably still be living in San Francisco and frustrated that I never took the leap to become the writer I had always dreamed of becoming.

How did we get here from starting out with the day in Athens?

Because although I'm still not "there" yet, I have learned that "there" is an imaginary place. It's that dream, future, fantasy place that, hold onto your hats, *doesn't actually exist.*

If I keep waiting for that perfect moment, the glorious scene (usually influenced by movies) where, I don't know, fireworks go off in the distance as I type the last words of my award-winning novel while I sip whiskey (I don't even like whiskey!) on the veranda of my lake house while the water ripples the shimmering moonbeams …

Stop! Pleases stop!

I'm in Athens, I'm writing, I have many books, I'm with my family, we're eating Gyros, we're doing bike tours. I even managed to skip dinner the first night, wake up early, meditate, and write a few chapters.

No fireworks. No lake. No dream as I had envisioned at some point in the past.

Yet here I am living some form of that dream in the present day.

> *Dear Reader,*
> *This is one of the hardest things about being a writer (or*
> *creator). Getting the message across or through or*
> *getting it to really land as I hope it will or can.*
> *There are tidbits in life, in chapters of books, in scenes in*
> *movies, or moment in real life, that we somehow never*
> *forget. They sink in. We can't forget them even if we*
> *wanted to.*
> *This is an important chapter.*
> *One of the biggest reasons I write books at all is to share*
> *experiences that I have had, mistakes I have made, and*
> *of course successes I have enjoyed, with you so that you*
> *recognize the mistakes more quickly (and still make*
> *them but realize what they are and move on), to take*
> *the chances, to dare to create, and get to the successes*
> *more quickly and hopefully less painfully than I did.*
> *The Author*

Back to the title of this chapter:

Live (A Little) Of Your Future Dream Life Now

Please, pretty please, don't wait for the fireworks and the lake and the veranda.

Of course, dream your dreams, envision them for the future, but then let them arrive in pieces, probably not in order, and certainly not exactly as you had envisioned it.

I can honest and truly say I am living my dream right now. Today. Here in this apartment in Athens as I type on my broken laptop and a woman across the way is over watering her plants to the extent that she's washing the cars below.

I'm writing. I'm creating.

I'm taking this moment, this chapter, to remind myself, to remind you, to capture, to sneak in, to secretly and maybe quietly recognize, relish and celebrate the tiny wins, the successes that resemble if only in the slightest way, the dreams of your past that are happening in the present day of your real life.

This book has, ideally, become A Clear Path Forward offering up a methodology, a roadmap, a path for you to get some clarity, take some action, and build some confidence so that you may live a little of your future dream life right now.

- **Possible:** live your future life in the past
- **Impossible:** live your entire future life in the present
- **Repossible:** live your future life in the present (if only a tiny bit)

P.S. That bar last night with the Ouzo was one of the most beautiful bars I have ever seen in my life. I'll share a photo in the bonus content.

PART IV

YOU DON'T HAVE TO INTERMITTENT FAST

"Nothing tastes as good as this feels."

— BRADLEY CHARBONNEAU

13

I AM NOT A DOCTOR

NO, REALLY. I HAVEN'T EVEN ACTED AS ONE ON TV.

> "Periodic fasting can help clear up the mind and strengthen the body and the spirit."
>
> — EZRA TAFT BENSON

Here, I just found this (and altered it a bit) on the Internet. Where, you know, you can believe everything you read. Not like here, in a book, from some author (who isn't a doctor).

NOT MEDICAL ADVICE: The information, including but not limited to, text, graphics, images and other material contained in this book are for informational purposes only. No material in this book is intended to be a substitute for professional medical advice, diagnosis or treatment. Always seek the advice of your physician or other qualified health care provider with any questions you may have regarding a medical condition or treatment and before undertaking a new health care regimen, and never disregard professional medical advice or delay in

> *seeking it because of something you have read in this book.*

Are we good?

Pretty much the extent of what I'm suggesting in this book is to skip dinner and stop eating at 4 PM until the next morning.

Remember, I'm not a doctor.

If you want to know crazy stuff I've done, I'm going to put it in the bonus content (see lesson called "I Am Not a Doctor"). I also put in there any resources on intermittent fasting I have used—especially since I'm consciously trying to not give advice on it in this book!

- **Possible:** fast without knowing anything about it
- **Impossible:** get all of the right answers from the right people at the right time
- **Repossible:** consult your trusted medical practitioner

14

IT'S 5:34

I'M ALIVE

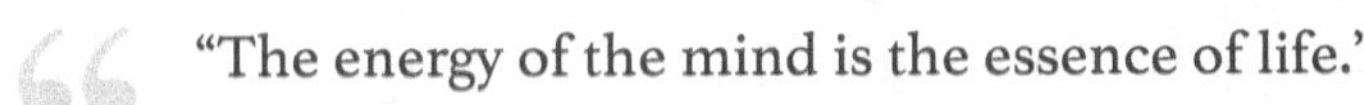

"The energy of the mind is the essence of life."

— ARISTOTLE

I want to quickly get my thoughts onto the page while they're fresh.

Fresh.

It's the perfect word.

It's early for sure.

But I've had "enough" sleep. I woke up a few minutes ago without an alarm clock. I opened my eyes and within seconds felt awake, alive, even energetic.

The night before, actually now three nights in a row, I followed a similar pattern:

1. I stopped eating at 4 PM
2. I only drank water or tea afterwards (actually, quite a lot)
3. I went to bed earlier than normal (before 11, ideally before 10)

4. I woke up early (usually before 6 AM)
5. I felt full of energy, immediately awake, ready to go with my day and full of creative and positive ideas

A few weeks ago I went to southern Spain to spend five days with longtime friends for a birthday. It was fabulous: endless tapas, sunshine, red wine, walks on the beach, flowing Cava, hikes in the mountains, late nights, lots of laughter and cheer.

But whew. Those mornings? Those were tough. Not quite to the hangover level, but slow going and thinking things like, "Ooh, I should take it a bit easier on the alcohol tonight."

Don't get me wrong: we had a fantastic time. It was special, even powerful (with late-night animated discussions), and I'd do it all again in a heartbeat. And plan to.

Yet this feeling at 5:34 AM?

If I have to compare? It's better.

Do I have to choose?

Not necessarily. I can have both. Well, not in the same day (or even week) but maybe last week was Spain and this week is intermittent fasting.

But if I did have to choose only one?

The decision is a no-brainer: this one. Intermittent fasting.

The power, the energy, the creativity I feel right now before the sun is even up, before I'm dressed, before my day—or anyone's day—has even started?

This is worth more than Cava and tapas. Even better than a good time with old friends.

Sound crazy?

It is a little bit.

And I would never have believed such a thing coming from anyone, no matter how much I trusted, believed or admired them.

There was just no way that being up early with such energy could be better than hanging out with friends.

Do I have to choose?

No.

Can I have both?
Yes.

- **Possible:** eat and sleep
- **Impossible:** don't eat and don't sleep
- **Repossible:** eat less and sleep less

15

MEAT AND ALCOHOL

OH SURE, THEY'RE FUN!

"Energy and persistence conquer all things."

— BENJAMIN FRANKLIN

There are certainly other things we eat and drink that I'm sure intermittent fasting experts will tell us all about but there are two here that I have noticed disproportionately affect my sleep and then my meditation and my creating.

Meat and alcohol.

Here's a weird one. Although maybe it's just me. If I eat quite a bit of meat later at night and go to sleep within a few hours, I will usually have nightmares.

Not even the fun nightmares that are a little scary but these nightmares that are not fun.

In the morning after meat and alcohol, like right now as I write this, it's not even that I'm hungover or even have a headache but there is something of a dullness, a lack of sharpness or clarity, that isn't only in my stomach or gut but somehow is throughout my body.

The quote at the beginning of the fasting section of this book is something I try to remember as I'm out and about and eating and drinking and merrymaking.

 "Nothing tastes as good as this feels."

— ME

Yet I'd like to be clear with my intention for this book. If I ever become the guy who says "You can never do that!" or that you must eat two kilos of broccoli every morning and can never have a yummy Chai or go for a drink with your friends, or especially this one, if I become the guy who's at the restaurant and makes a huge fuss about how my meal will be prepared and what to put on the side and to leave out this and add more of that and all at the same time sending out a message to everyone at the table that the way I'm doing it is the best and probably only way and if they don't do it like I'm doing it then they are all big losers and say it all with a smile as if this is all normal and the waitress doesn't secretly want to murder me.

OK, whew. Glad I got that out.

I don't want to be that guy.

Yep, this chapter is about meat and alcohol and when I eat and drink those things my mornings are less clear and productive and happy and blah blah blah.

But meat and alcohol (or whatever it is that you really enjoy) are fun. I love a good burger (although the veggie burger industry is really stepping up their game!).

And my friends and I had a rollicking good time in Spain last month. I'm not giving that up anytime soon (READ: never).

What foods and drinks put a damper on your morning? Anything that really clearly makes a difference? If you'd like to share, head over to go.repossible.com/ydht-bonus and find Meat and Alcohol and leave a comment.

- **Possible:** go vegetarian

- **Impossible:** the veggie burger at In-N-Out Burger (HINT: they just take out the meat patty!)
- **Repossible:** everything in moderation

16

WATER

IT'S NOT JUST FOR BREAKFAST ANYMORE

 "Water is the driving force of all nature."

— LEONARDO DA VINCI

Have I mentioned I'm not a doctor?

Or a meditation guru?

Or a New York Times best-selling author?

Yet here I am.

- Light
- Joyful
- Fulfilled

I might chalk it up to:

- Water
- An Eyemask
- A Keyboard

Remember that chapter where I wasn't selling you stuff? Let me not sell you more stuff you don't need.

Water.

I'm feeling the urge for yet another disclaimer.

> "I'm not a doctor. I get queasy at the sight of blood. I think water is a magical wonder medicine. Like I said, don't believe anything I say without consulting someone who knows what they're talking about and has shellacked diplomas from reputable institutions of education in every profile photo."

> — THE AUTHOR

But back to water.

If you don't add soda syrup (I do this regularly ... don't do this regularly) to your water, it's really all you need for intermittent fasting.

Did you read the disclaimer?

Please go read books or watch reputable videos about intermittent fasting so you don't break something.

But I'm here to say that I Love Water.

I drink a liter every morning. I've even made something of a ritual of it. If it's basketball season, I'll watch a 7-minute NBA highlight on YouTube and drink my water. If I haven't finished my water when the video is done, I chug down the rest of it.

If you don't do anything else in this book, this one tiny little thing, every single day, has been such a wonderful discovery for me. It cleanses me (literally ...), it energizes me, and I actually like drinking it.

Bonus Water Tips

You read the disclaimer, right?

When I'm skipping a dinner, I drink more water. My family thinks it's fairly anti-social (it is) but I'll sit there at the family dinner with my bottle or glass of water while they eat.

Sometimes, I'm hungry and want to eat. Most of the time, when I'm really into my fasting, it's fairly easy.

I'll go to bed early. I might have another bottle of sparkling water. Yes, I know, some say don't drink so much sparkling water. Have you read the disclaimer? I'm not saying you should do this, I'm saying I do this and it works for me. Your mileage may vary.

Another Water Secret

This one is a little silly and some might even find it annoying but if I drink quite a bit of water at night, say, more than a liter, I'll have to wake up earlier to go to the bathroom. If it's past, say, 4 or 5 in the morning and I didn't have dinner the night before, guess what happens? I'll get up.

By the time I'm back to bed, more often than not, I'm feeling rather awake, usually rather awesome, and I'll head downstairs for a meditation.

See how fasting and water and meditation work together?

Then guess what happens?

I slept better, I'm up earlier, I have some water even before my meditation (so I'm not hungry although I'm rarely hungry so early), then if I'm really feeling like a rockstar, I won't even have my sugary, yummy, delicious Chai, but I'll keep going on the water and get maybe just a single chapter done.

It can be that simple.

If it doesn't sound that simple, check out the chapter about rituals and either use that or create your own set of steps (a ritual) and do that.

- **Possible:** drink when you're thirsty
- **Impossible:** drink beverages with water in them
- **Repossible:** drink (lots of) water

A Little Bonus Story About the Author

When I first met my wife, we both wanted to travel. In fact, it's the mutual love for travel that brought us together. It keeps us together as we still travel as much as possible.

We were living in Amsterdam and we went on a weekend trip to Belgium. Then we went for a longer trip to France. We both wanted more.

We talked and dreamed and didn't let go—of the idea of travel or the idea of traveling together.

We thought about going through Europe for a month. How much time could we get off work? Or three months! Then we'd have to quit our jobs.

If we're going to quit our jobs, we might as well go six months. If we do such a big trip, something we might never do again, we might as well go a full year.

So we did.

A constant through those twelve months through Africa and Asia was water.

In the countries where the quality of tap water wasn't so good and you couldn't even always trust the bottled water, we used our portable water purifier.

It was a little device, about the size of a liter bottle. You put in the not-so-clean water, pump it a bunch of times for several minutes, and you'd have about a liter of clean water.

It was usually hot where we were and we were sweating all the time so we drank untold liters of water every single day.

That meant pumping daily, sometimes hourly.

At some point, we were so bored with plain water that we started a search for little tablets to give it some flavor—any flavor—rather than just the water.

But still, the water was our daily bread—almost literally.

We didn't need to intermittent fast back then. We had 17-hour bus rides that provided the same results.

As for meditation? See the 17-hour bus rides.

Creating?

We didn't have laptops (or even mobile phones) so we were old school: pens and notebooks.

As I write this here today, in the book that has become so much more than I thought it would be, I see the similarities from the past with the present day.

Back then it was long bus rides, lots of water, little food, and maybe a rumbling snooze on a rickety bus in Zimbabwe and a frenzy of trying to write it all down with my 4-color BIC pen.

Today I have to make more of a ritual of it. The intermittent fasting, the waking up early, the eye mask, the guided meditation, writing, then hitting record on my phone.

It's a different time, a much different place, and a different mindset.

But the ritual is there. The water is there.

The results are there.

The means are right there, available and free to you every single day.

Water.

Now, I'm going to go see if Luca is awake and see how the Warriors did last night.

- **Possible:** other drinks
- **Impossible:** no water
- **Repossible:** water

17

5:55

CLARITY, COURAGE, AND CONFIDENCE

> "The best way to make your dreams come true is to wake up."
>
> — PAUL VALERY

As I sit down here on this Wednesday morning, the sun rising outside, the birds chirping like it's going out of style, I smile as I type.

Now I completely, absolutely, and wholeheartedly understand if you are cringing right now and saying something like:

> "Oh sure, Mr. Happy Morning Person. Yeah, you go. You do you. You wake up early, start typing and SMILE. Ridiculous."
>
> — MAYBE YOU. MAYBE ME ON MANY OTHER DAYS

It's Wednesday. I've now skipped dinner Monday and Tuesday nights. Not 100% not a bite of anything, but pretty close.

Last night, I made dinner for Luca (he was the only one home with me) and it was some steak, a pasta with tomato sauce and some rich, old Dutch cheese, even a few slices of a dry sausage we had from Italy, and ... hungry yet?

Yet, I managed to not have a single bite.

> **PRO TIP:** *I'd wager that most of what I eat comes while making food, especially dinner, for my family. I just have a bite of this and make a little snack of that. It's one of the hardest things I know, but to not have a bite while I'm preparing a meal is tough. Real tough.*

I looked at the clock this morning: 5:55. I'm not a huge numerology person but still, it's fun.

I knew I had the energy to wake up immediately.

The birds are going wild outside as the sun is starting to wake up, too. It's late March and spring is springing.

I got up, went downstairs, wrote "5:55" in my notebook on my desk, arranged my mediation station, and picked a random meditation from Dr. Joe (I found, "Embracing the Goddess Within," which was perfect as I need to send some love inwards). Towards the end of the meditation, he says something about keeping this energy, this love for the duration of the ... I thought he was going to say meditation but he said day.

If I had one dream for this book, one dream for myself, for you, it would be this: to hold onto the power, the energy, the love I/we feel during meditation and spread it throughout the day. That's my goal, my dream.

I finished my meditation and didn't turn on the TV (the Warriors have been playing and they're not doing so well ... and it's March so that means March Madness so Luca and I watch quite a bit of NCAA basketball) but I came straight here and typed 5:55 as my chapter title.

Then I started writing.

Here in this single chapter. Here with yet another oddball chapter title, I bury, I hide, I secretly share with you what You Don't Have To do (but if you WANT to, if you DARE to, you can achieve what you want). I believe you can achieve pretty much anything you want with the simple, easy-to-replicate formula in this book:

1. Fast
2. Meditate
3. Create

This chapter is living proof, actual words written after fasting and meditating that **would have been a different chapter** had I not fasted, and meditated and sat down to create.

Remember, I started Monday, two days ago so maybe it's not just a single night of fasting but a few in a row. Frankly, the more, the better.

At some point, you'll experience the energy, the power, the clarity and you'll want to do more and more.

These simple steps and I have:

1. Clarity
2. Courage
3. Confidence

Ooh, those are too good to pass up—and I can't keep away from alliteration.

Let's expand.

1. **Clarity:** to know what to do (and when and how)
2. **Courage:** to dare to start
3. **Confidence:** to persevere and finish

Boom, boom, boom.

I didn't have those three words this morning at 5:55.

It's now 7:11 and I do.

> *PRO TIP: In a way, I could call it a day. It's 7:11 in the*
> *morning. I have my chapter, my output, my creation. If*
> *I did this every single day, I could have 365 chapters in*

> *a year or just 30 in a single month. There's a book a*
> *month. Or a project or a business or a _______ fill in*
> *what you'd like to accomplish. Boom. Boom. Boom.*

Do you hear that boom? It's that rumble in your heart.

As I type these words, I kid you not, I have butterflies and shivers running through my chest. I smile as I type this as this is where I live, this is where I thrive.

There's your roadmap. It's so simple it can be hard to believe.

Hidden in a chapter called just 5:55 in a book with an oddball title. **Clarity. Courage. Confidence.**

Now, I'm going to go see if Luca is awake and see how the Warriors did last night.

- **Possible:** wake up early and energized once
- **Impossible:** wake up early and energized every single day
- **Repossible:** wake up early and energized regularly

P.S. This chapter which I wrote on some random Wednesday morning and I thought was "just going to be another chapter" has not only become the heading of a section of this book but a three-word mantra (clarity, courage, confidence) for many of the projects I'm working on. In other words, in creating, we don't always know what we're creating and we don't always even recognize it at the time, but it could be something, it might turn into something but if we do nothing, if we create nothing, then that won't turn into anything.

18

21:09

ATHENS, GREECE. I HAVE A CHOICE. RIGHT NOW. #GYROS

> "There's usually a choice. It's usually yours."
>
> — BRADLEY CHARBONNEAU

I hadn't planned to make this section so much about times of the day.

But as I write books, I try to think about myself as the reader and often say this, even aloud:

> "If I can get a single nugget of actionable information from this book, it's a win."
>
> — ME, AS BOTH AUTHOR AND READER

I'm writing this the morning after. I seem to wake up without an alarm at 6:36 on a regular basis. This morning, too. Even on holiday, even after a full travel day yesterday.

We arrived last night in Greece, in Athens. We got to our apartment around 9 PM and the boys were hungry. I was torn. As much as I couldn't wait to have a gyros (the sliced meat wrapped in a fresh pita bread and lathered up with mouth-tingling tzatziki sauce), I quietly hoped the boys would be too tired to go out so we could just go to sleep early, skip dinner, and wake up early to be fit and fresh for our e-bike tour of the city.

Clearly, the metabolism rates for teenagers and those who of us who no longer have the metabolism rate of teenagers is a cavern of difference.

Dearest Reader,

Please know that I completely understand that many choices I make are not normal or mainstream or what even my family chooses to do.

I bet I have a chapter in one of my books somewhere that says that this is also not my goal (normalcy, etc.).

I choose to be different, I choose to make a game of it all, to see if I can skip dinner, have a great sleep, wake up earlier than everyone, do my meditation, and write three chapters in my latest book (this one).

This is what I consider fun.

I didn't move to a hut in Nepal and give up on gyros and family and friends and Ouzo and sightseeing. On the contrary, I do all of that, too.

Too. Also. Maybe with even more spirit.

*Maybe it's **because** I play games with life and enjoy these "silly" things and maybe because I enjoy the silly things that the "normal" things are even more enjoyable.*

I don't know if any of that made sense but if you're thinking this isn't normal and you are seeking normal, I'm probably not your guy and this is probably not your book and you have the choice when I say, "You Don't Have To" to answer back, "I Won't."

The Author

Where were we? Oh yes, 21:09.

We'll be in Greece for seven or eight days. I have a chance this first night to secretly and quietly play my little game of intermittent fasting (followed by mediation and creation).

It's a safe bet I won't have the opportunity again this trip as we get into the rhythm of travel and I will fall into the flow of our days here.

Yet here's the message: **even if you can do one day in a week where you fast and meditate and create and the other six days you do your regular thing, it's a win.**

Remember, my goal isn't to eventually do more days of the week to the point where I don't have dinner seven days a week. Not at all.

Another book I'm working on is called "Frequency." The subtitle will be something like "How Often to Do What—And Why."

Just like here. What if just one day/night per week, you tried this? Not necessarily on holiday (although I have to state that sometimes on holiday is actually easier because your regular routines are already different) but in any regular week.

Maybe pick a certain day of the week. I have been weighing myself on the scale on Fridays so Thursday evenings became something of a default night to skip dinner. Then I made a *routine* of it, a *habit* of it, even a *ritual* of it.

I hope you can appreciate how this chapter has evolved—and this is exactly my point, my goal with "Create." I started this chapter with just a simple story of how it was 21:09 and I made the No Gyro choice.

It then cascaded into a better night's sleep, waking up early, a simple yet good meditation, and writing this (and two other!) chapters in this book.

- Simple.
- Easy.
- Simple and easy.
- Simple but not easy.

This chapter, this exercise probably falls for most of us in the Simple But Not Easy category.

Until, of course, you practice and eventually it becomes both simple and easy.

- **Possible:** have half a gyros now and feel half awesome in the morning
- **Impossible:** have a gyros now and feel awesome in the morning
- **Repossible:** have a gyros tomorrow

I'll put a photo of my gyros in the bonus content.

PART V

YOU DON'T HAVE TO MEDITATE

"You should sit in meditation for 20 minutes a day. Unless you're too busy, then you should sit for an hour."

— OLD ZEN SAYING

19

I AM NOT A GURU

YOUR BEST GURU IN YOUR FUTURE SELF

> "When there are thoughts, it is distraction: when there are no thoughts, it is meditation."
>
> — RAMANA MAHARSHI

I used the quote above because I don't agree with it. In fact, that's what I'm shooting for in this section of the book about meditation: do what works for you.

There are currently more than a dozen books in my Repossible series. I'm often asked which is my favorite (Create) or most important (Decide) or which was the hardest to write (Surrender).

But the book, the concept, that I believe was and is the most important element of all of the books? Meditate.

Did you catch that title? I don't wear an orange robe and I'm not even sure where Nepal is. I'm not a guru.

Meditation has done for me what nothing else has.

Yep, I love creating and I'm a huge fan and proponent. I think it's the key to starting with change.

But to work through, to get the clarity, to reach higher levels. As the author of this book I can tell you something you might find hard to believe coming from the author of the book you're reading: you're not going to find the answers to your life's questions in this book. Or in any book for that matter. Or in any course or program or workshop.

The answers are, and I know how cliché this is, within. You have the answers.

Sure, read the books, read this book, listen to me, listen to others, but mostly, after it's all taken in, you've read all of the books, followed all of the gurus, taken all of the workshops and retreated on the most glorious of the retreats, listen to yourself.

 "But Bradley, how can I listen to myself? All I hear is noise!"

Not only am I not your meditation guru but I don't want to be.

I'll give you one name here but I will also be updating the bonus content (go.repossible.com/ydht-bonus) more than I can update this book so have a look there under this chapter title (I Am Not A Guru) and I'll share any other resources I come across there.

Find your guru. Be your own guru.

But above all, figure out how you can best meditate.

- **Possible:** try
- **Impossible:** banish all thoughts for an hour
- **Repossible:** figure out how meditation works best for you

P.S. The one name I'll share here from my experience since 2014 is Joe Dispenza. I'll offer up more in the bonus content.

20

ALL OF HUMANITY'S PROBLEMS

WAIT. SERIOUSLY? THAT SOUNDS LIKE A LOT OF PROBLEMS.

"All of humanity's problems stem from man's inability to sit quietly in a room alone."

— BLAISE PASCAL

The French philosopher wrote that quote in the 1600's.

They didn't have cell phones, TVs, and not even Instagram.

Yet the quote keeps coming up. I did a Google search and it's quoted on a regular basis.

Could it be true?

I'm going to do something crazy this chapter. I'm going to leave it right here.

Sure, I could write more and more. I could weigh both sides, find more opinions and arguments for and against.

Or I could just leave it with you.

Here's my little challenge for you. It's tiny. It won't hurt. Much.

Say the quote out loud.

Then close your eyes and say it out loud again. Replace man with woman if you like.

Then one more time.

Then one more time not audibly but only in your mind.

"All of humanity's problems" sounds like a tall order.

What if we did the "sit quietly alone" exercise for just one tiny problem of our own.

See how that goes.

Then move onto *all of humanity*.

Or not.

Because ... *all of humanity* begins with you.

- **Possible:** sit
- **Impossible:** sit quietly alone forever
- **Repossible:** sit quietly alone

21

NORMAL MEDITATION
I GUESS THAT'S A THING

"We meditate to get good at life, not to get good at meditation."

— EMILY FLETCHER

'm writing this chapter after I wrote Not Sarah and Dawn. Had I read those chapters even a few short years ago, I would have thought:

"Whoa, this Bradley Charbonneau guy is out there!"

— ME, A FEW YEARS AGO

I wanted to write this chapter to first bring us back to earth (because you'll see we're flying high in the next few chapters!).

I get lots of questions about meditation and since I've been doing it now since 2014, it's one of those things that I can't really explain very well because it's just become second nature to me.

Like explaining to someone who has never ridden a bicycle.

 "Well, let's see. First there's the idea of balance and gravity. Then there's the physics of motion."

Yeah, good luck with that.

Yet, I feel about the same with meditation.

Here's my no-roadmap, no-structure, no-messing-around take on it as I now see it:

"Sit down, close your eyes, and fly away."

See? That's just weird. It also doesn't help you, dear reader, who may or may not have much experience with meditation and you're going to say something like:

 "Gee, thanks, Mr. I Am Not a Guru. At least give me a hint."

Let's start at the end.

For me, the goal of meditation is usually clarity. Remember, I do feel bold enough to disagree with the quote at the top of the I Am Not a Guru chapter:

 "When there are thoughts, it is distraction: when there are no thoughts, it is meditation."

— RAMANA MAHARSHI

I really like people like Emily Fletcher (reread that quote at the top of this chapter) who are practical, don't have purple feathers, and usually don't mention flying unicorns.

I want clarity.

I also want courage and confidence.

I think courage and confidence can come from clarity.

I'm walking a bit of a tightrope in this book because I'm consciously trying to NOT guide you or "teach" you about meditation yet I'm saying it's so important. What I'm trying to do there is to guide you to find someone to listen to in a guided meditation that resonates with you.

Here's my suggestion. You could even start on YouTube. It's free. Search for a guided meditation that's under 20 minutes or 30 max, find a place where you won't be bothered by anything or anyone, listen with your best headphones or ear buds, ideally put on an eye mask, and see what happens.

Follow the guide. If they have you walking on a beach or through a meadow, just go with it.

Here's my Secret Pro Tip: in a way, they're distracting you with the beach or the meadow. Yes, the goal is to clear your mind of the junk, the regular stuff, the grocery list.

Often when you're trying to get rid of the shopping list and you're trying to focus on the sandy beach and the turquoise waters they're describing your thoughts will wander elsewhere. Maybe they'll be on the beach. Great.

But maybe they'll be on something else. If it's back to the shopping list, let that go. We're looking for something bigger, more important. But it might not seem important.

In the chapter 5:55, I started a meditation without any goal or intention and came up with a three-word subtitle for a future book (and a section of this book).

How about this: do your best to let the junk ideas fall out of your head, listen to the guided meditation, try to visualize the beach (or the whatever), and let whatever comes in come in.

Then play with it.

Play is an important word and verb here.

Meditation shouldn't be a struggle. Yep, it might be in the beginning but soon enough and if you let it, it will be more playful.

Check out my resources in the Bonus Content under the heading I Am Not A Guru as I'll add to that with some more guidance about mediation.

Now that I've got the "Normal Meditation" out of the way, come fly with me in the zany chapters titled Not Sarah and Dawn.

In case you think I'm crazy, it's only recently that I would even have dared to publish such private experiences I have had with my eyes closed.

But honestly? That's the fun of it. When it's fun, when it's play and wild and mystical and unexpected, at some point, when you get past judgment, you just want to share in the hopes that others can experience the joy and clarity that meditation brings.

Let it be fun. Let it be easy.

- **Possible:** wonder whether or not we can really banish all thoughts from our minds
- **Impossible:** 10-day silent meditation retreat (in a weekend)
- **Repossible:** find your flow

22

NOT SARAH

PAST LIFE REGRESSION LIGHT

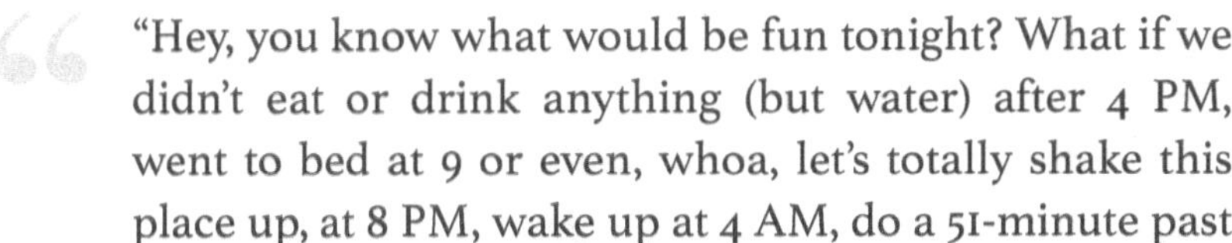

"If you don't have time to meditate for an hour every-day, you should meditate for two hours."

— ZEN PROVERB

It's Friday morning. I weigh myself each Friday. #ritual I didn't have dinner last night (see previous sentence). I was up fairly early (5:34), felt good, and had the thought of changing what has been my Sunday morning ritual of doing a Past Life Regression to Friday mornings.

My best meditations come after a night (ideally, more than just one night) of fasting. As pleasant and peaceful as Sunday mornings can be, Saturday nights aren't the best time to propose the following to my wife:

"Hey, you know what would be fun tonight? What if we didn't eat or drink anything (but water) after 4 PM, went to bed at 9 or even, whoa, let's totally shake this place up, at 8 PM, wake up at 4 AM, do a 51-minute past

life regression, record an audio recap of that meditation, and then write a chapter (or several) of a book?
You think? Wouldn't that be a blast?"

— NO ONE SAID TO NO SPOUSE EVER

So, yeah. There's that.

How about Thursday night and Friday mornings!? How about not asking my wife to join me!?

Done.

This morning, I found a new past life regression guided meditation (see below for link) that was only 22 minutes long.

I'm working on a bunch of really fun things right now (Easiest Book Ever 10-Day Challenge, this book, and working with two part-
ners on what will probably become my "Repossible" Coaching Program or "Brand New U." or "Boost Your Brand With a Book" ... wow, that slipped in there quickly, guess I really am rather excited about working on them!) so I didn't really feel like spending a whole hour on a meditation.

When will I learn?
PRO TIP: *Never.*

In case I lost you, the conversation I'm having with myself above is **if it's possible to do in a 22-minute meditation the same thing as in a 51-minute meditation.** (I'll put both videos in the bonus content.)

The quick answer? No.

The long answer. Yes.

It depends on what you want to accomplish.

This morning, for example, it took me several minutes to get all of my To Do List out of my head.

Then, she guided us through only one scene and when I was settling in and seeing and experiencing more, it was ending.

If I had been more focused and prepared, might I have benefitted more sooner? Absolutely.

But hi there! Welcome to reality.

Even the guy writing a book about fasting, meditating, and creating doesn't always want to do the 51-minute meditation.

There you have it, your free pass to not always do the longer one.

But that's just it: not **always**.

I have a book in me called "Frequency" and it's about **How Often to Do What and Why**. It would help in this situation here to explain or rationalize how often to do the 22-minute meditation (e.g. daily) and how often to do the deeper, 51-minute one (e.g. weekly) and then how often to do the group, 3-hour meditation (monthly).

Wouldn't such a roadmap with a schedule be handy? Yeah, so I need to finish that book.

But back to Not Sarah.

Usually, in the past life regressions I get a very clear name of the person who is a part of my past life. Even with spelling!

This time, she was clear, her name was *not* Sarah.

I even called out to her and the conversation went like this:

"Sarah?"
"Not Sarah."

She was even chiding me, although in a friendly way, that I wasn't spending enough time with her this morning so I wasn't going to get her name. She mentioned towards the end that I could return to her to get her name should I wish.

I describe what my experience was better in audio and the link to that audio is below so I will leave you with this bit of wisdom probably from a used car salesman:

"You get what you pay for."

— USED CAR SALESMAN (PROBABLY)

The quote that opens this chapter is relevant. Having done a 10-day silent retreat where we didn't talk, read, or even engage in eye contact with other people, I can say from experience that we don't need to meditate hours (and hours) every single day unless you're really going for the whole monk thing.

But that's not what I'm going for. You?

I'm going for:

> *"How can I bring some of the beauty, energy, love and power that I get in my meditations into my regular, daily, normal life?"*

That's what I'm going for.

What are you going for?

Not Sarah will get me there but not as quickly as Sarah.

I feel like I've been teasing around the idea of a longer and "better" past life regression meditation so I'll cover that in the next chapter.

> *Yet Another **PRO TIP**: it is not lost on me that even though I'm (kind of) saying here that a 22-minute meditation wasn't as good as a 51-minute meditation, keep in mind that I got two chapters for this book out of it. So, what are your goals and dreams for your meditations? Mind-boggling, orgasmic, out-of-body mystical experiences every single morning? Or Not Sarah? Or, don't forget this option: no meditation at all.*

There's usually a choice. It's usually yours.

Where have I heard that? ;) Decide.

- **Possible:** 22 minutes of meditation in hopes of getting 51 minutes worth
- **Impossible:** 22 hours of meditation daily (well, OK, possible!)

- **Repossible:** 51 minutes on Fridays, 22 minutes other days

You can find my recorded version of this chapter and the 22-minute and 51-minute Past Life Regression YouTube videos at the bonus content for YDHT at go.repossible.com/ydht-bonus.

23

DAWN

THE REALLY WEIRD PART IS HOW THIS IS GETTING LESS WEIRD

 "If you change the way you look at things, the things you look at change."

— WAYNE DYER

DISCLAIMER: There is no disclaimer.

Oh me, oh my, dear reader.

It's 2022 as I write this.

I'm 100% sure that if I had read this chapter or listened to the 17-minute audio recording called "Dawn," I not only wouldn't have believed it but I probably would have thought that the person recording it was either a wacko, a witch, or (can I find another W word?) a *wonder*.

There. I said it.

Remember, back just a few short years ago, I would have said such a person was way woo woo (wow, really going for the whole W thing here—and winning!) or I just wouldn't need to associate with that person (mostly because I'd think they were way woo woo and too far from reality).

Yet here we are just a few years later and not only am I embracing that person with the whacked-out stories of fantastical, mystical, and mosaic-filled meditations, but I AM that person.

Then, as if that weren't enough, I'm not quietly wondering what is going on and why and then proceeding to hide out and tell no one for fear of the judgment of the type of person I was just a few short years ago, but I'm saying it out loud, to myself, to you, and in this book.

No Disclaimer Here

There are a certain few friends who will be proud of me for NOT making a disclaimer at this point.

At the point where I'm going to get "weirder" than you already thought I was.

In the past, I might say, "DISCLAIMER: things are about to get weird. If you're not into weird, please stop reading now."

Nope. No disclaimer.

Things are about to get weird and I'm not only not going to deny it or hide from it but I'm shouting it from the rooftops ... or at least the literary version of putting it all into a chapter of my book.

Dawn

All of this above is a prelude for you to meet Dawn. Dawn who I met in my past-life regression meditation.

> *Ha, I'm literally smiling and even chuckling to myself as I type this because I realize how much I'm coming out of my shell, out of the mystical closet, and how little I care about the judgment and care mostly that I can convey the the clarity, courage, and confidence that these expe-riences provide me and for you, even though You Don't Have To, to benefit from them, too.*

As I type this, I have Deva Premal in my ears on my favorite head-phones turned on low volume as I listen to my own 17-minute recording titled Dawn and the sun is rising and I love that I'm sharing this with you.

Quick Notes from the Audio

- **Mosaic** (we aren't just individuals from the past but a mosaic, a combination, of past individuals)
- **Oxygen mask** (take care of yourself first)
- **Treasure Map** (roadmap, figure out what to do, map out what to do to help others get there)

Mosaic

I'm not going to be able to get across in this chapter as clearly as I did immediately in my post-meditation audio recording.

But to get the words out as best I can, our past lives are made up of a mosaic of past lives. So it's not that our past lives are just a single person and we are now the future version of that one person but that person is a mosaic and the "I" of today is one little element of that person.

So today, we are another mosaic of tiny little pieces (souls? beings?) made up of many, many people from the past.

I wish I could draw this. But it's not a 1-to-1 ratio. It's a many-to-many ratio.

Oxygen Masks & Treasure Maps

Finally, in case this wasn't clear, remember that in addition to the crazy, mystical fun (which is *so much more fun* than Netflix or hallucinogenic drugs), we often can get out rational, real, and relevant (wow, the alliteration is on high alert in this chapter!) to our current lives (e.g. the oxygen masks and treasure maps).

Then, what I'm hoping from this chapter is **not** that you say:

"Gee, Bradley, that's really awesome for you that you meet up with Dawn and she answers all of your life's questions in a single morning but, yeah, that's never going to work for me."

— HOPEFULLY NOT YOU

But that you say, and I realize this is a bit of a stretch as I started out this chapter with how I wouldn't even believe my own self if my own self of just a few years ago heard this I wouldn't have even been interested.

But here's what I hope you think:

 "Gee, Bradley, that's super crazy that you have completely whacked out past-life regressions on a Sunday morning that seemingly change your life in a matter of an hour.

I've never even done a past-life regression nor do I really understand it.

But honestly, if you say you weren't into this stuff and never did it before just a few months ago, and now you're doing it and you're meeting women like Dawn who say, "Come back anytime." and tell you about mosaics, roadmaps for your clients, and oxygen masks to take care of yourself, well who is to say that I can't do this myself?

I can tell you. Not only is no one saying I **can't** do it myself, but you are here telling me I **can** do it myself.

So, thanks for that."

— MAYBE YOU

I now hope you're whispering to yourself, "I know I don't have to do this stuff but I quietly, maybe secretly, want to do this stuff."

If I can dare to do it and share it publicly in a book, you can start with daring to do it privately and telling no one but ... someone you might meet like Dawn.

- **Possible:** question weird
- **Impossible:** avoid weird
- **Repossible:** embrace (your new) weird

Listen to the 17-minute, post past life regression audio recap at the YDHT bonus content site, go.repossible.com/ydht-bonus. It's titled Dawn.

PART VI

YOU DON'T HAVE TO WRITE A BOOK

"You Must Write a Book"

— TITLE OF A REAL BOOK

24

THE BOOK I SHOULD WRITE

SHOULD, SUPPOSED TO, THINK I HAVE TO …

> "If you feel like there's something out there that you're supposed to be doing, if you have a passion for it, then stop wishing and just do it."
>
> — WANDA SYKES

Regarding the quote above, if you don't have a passion for it, then you're left with just "supposed to."

PRO TIP: If you do have a passion for it, see the next chapter, "The Book I Want to Write."

As I mentioned in the preface, I didn't have to write this book. In fact, I probably shouldn't even write it.

The books I "should" write are much more practical and immediately recognizable as helpful:

- **MailerLite for Authors:** Easy to Use Mailing Lists, Author Websites, and Surveys

- **Sell Your Ebooks and Audiobooks Direct:** Control Your Pricing and Coupons, Connect Directly with Your Fans, and Cash In on Direct Sales
- **The Traveler Mindset:** From Weekend Warrior to Vagabond of Riches

(OK, that last one sounds actually kind of interesting ... maybe that one will make the cut.)

Ha, those are actually on my list to write. But the book you have in your hands cut in line and made its way to the front because it has *want* and *passion* and not just *should*.

- **Possible:** write what you're supposed to write
- **Impossible:** write what you're supposed to write and kid yourself into thinking it's what you want to write
- **Repossible:** write what you want to write

25

THE BOOK I WANT TO WRITE
TRAVEL

"Your intellect may be confused, but your emotions will never lie to you."

— ROGER EBERT

There are chapters in this book where I mention that I was in Greece while writing.

I outlined a few books in the last chapter, "The Book I Should Write" so I have that list done. Just in case I run out of books I want to write or if, you know, reality sets in and, are you ready for this one? I write books I want to write, they don't sell anything, and then I think I have to write books I should write.

Oops, truth bomb!

Here comes a bit of a secret. I'm not sure I was experienced enough or maybe daring enough or gutsy or confident even just a few short years ago to state this but here goes.

I write the books I want to write.

I'm going to put it down below under Repossible because I think the Repossible option (as compared to Possible and Impossible) is the true answer, the answer you dream of, the one you wish comes true.

I'm going to say it again: I write the books I want to write.

> *BIG OLE DISCLAIMER: book authoring and success 101*
> *pro tip: books you want to write may or may not be the*
> *books people want to read (and, you know, pay for).*
> *However, dare I state from my vast experience of 32 books*
> *that I honest and truly will go so far as to say that I*
> *think the benefit we get from books from the emotional*
> *and psychological and even physiological perspective*
> *are more important for our wellbeing, our health, our*
> *joy, our purpose and meaning than those books that*
> *make us money.*
> *There, I said it.*
> *Written like a true author.*

Where were we? Oh yes, Greece.

I want to write about travel. How important it is. How, if I were elected master of time, space, and dimension, I would make it mandatory for each citizen of the planet to do a year abroad. It would be organized and paid for and the world would be a better place with just that simple act.

In fact, filling out my entire agenda of plans and missions ... nope, nothing else. Just that one. If every single person were "forced" to travel the world or, better yet, travel and live in a place for a while (I'm not talking about staying in fancy hotels, BTW), there would be less need for much of a further political agenda.

There you have it. My plan to rule (or well, more like un-rule) the world.

All inside of a book called Travel.

What's the book you want to write?

Not the one you think you're supposed to, but the one you can't not write?

Come over to the bonus content (go.repossible.com/ydht-bonus), find the post titled The Book I Want to Write and leave a comment.

- **Possible:** write the book you want to write
- **Impossible:** write any book and say it's the one you wanted to write
- **Repossible:** write the book you can't not write

26

AT FIRST, DON'T SUCCEED

I KNOW THAT'S NOT HOW IT GOES BUT ROLL WITH ME HERE FOR A MINUTE.

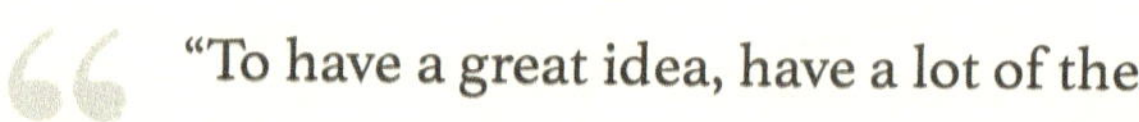 "To have a great idea, have a lot of them."

— THOMAS A. EDISON

Just in case the title of this chapter didn't quite make the landing I was shooting for and your parents never said this to you over and over as you crashed and burned trying (and failing) at whatever it was you were going for, the real quote is:

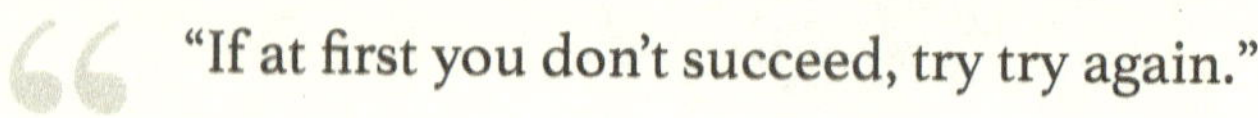 "If at first you don't succeed, try try again."

— EVERY PARENT EVER

Let's take it back to Mr. Edison and turn the equation into a math challenge.

What are the odds of succeeding the first time?

50/50, right?

You either fail or you succeed?

What are the odds that, hold onto your hats here, that you succeed one time out of 100?

If each individual attempt is 50/50, yes, of course, it's statistically possible to fail 100 times in a row, but if we stick to 50/50 for a moment and yet you don't know WHICH of the 100 attempts will be a success, I would suggest that the chance of just a single success in the 100 is 50 times greater than 50/50.

Remember, we're not saying you need to succeed 50 times in the 100 tries.

Just one.

Just a single success.

I spent 9 years NOT writing a book. Guess how many books I wrote? Yep. Zero.

Then I spent the next 6 years writing 31 books. Guess how many are successes?

Want to know the number I care about more than how many were successes?

How much fun did I have, how much joy, bliss, accomplishment and confidence did I experience by succeeding just that once?

Back to Thomas Edison.

 "To have a great idea, have a lot of them."

— THOMAS A. EDISON

So which idea of the 100 was the good one? Would you like to play roulette, put all of your 100 chips on one number and hope it hits?

Or would you rather play 100 times with a single chip and see how that goes?

Also, it's more fun that way and you might get to meet some of your fellow players and they usually bring around free drinks.

OK, I've gone from Thomas Edison to math class to a casino and free cocktails.

See what happens when I "have a lot of ideas?" They build on each other, they grow, they interact.

I've had fun writing just this chapter. It started out only with that quote from Edison and look where we've arrived.

I'm ready for a cocktail about now. You?

- **Possible:** try
- **Impossible:** succeed first
- **Repossible:** at first, don't succeed

27

(BUT) THE LETTER "T" DOESN'T WORK SO WELL

I'M GOING TO CREATE NO MATTER WHAT

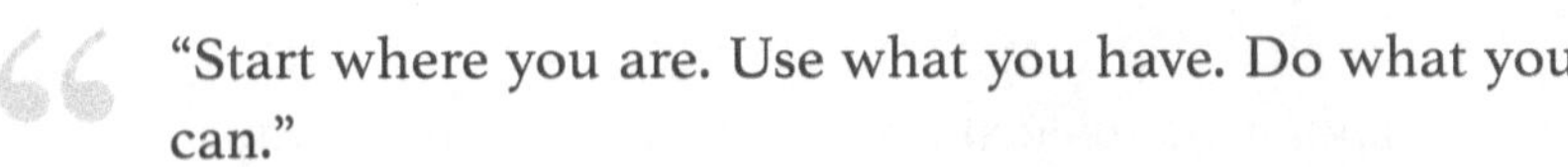

"Start where you are. Use what you have. Do what you can."

— ARTHUR ASHE

I'm typing this on a 2012 MacBook Air. It was my first Mac and it cost (what I thought was) a lot of money and I used it almost daily for more than eight years.

It still works. Obviously, as I'm typing on it!

But I can no longer update the operating system and if I have too many things open, it really slows down and the battery is basically worthless so I always have to have it plugged in.

I bring it when I'm traveling somewhere I'm a little less sure is safe or I think it might get stolen or fall into a river.

The worst part about it is that letter "T" key has pretty much dislocated.

I just counted and there were thirteen uses of the letter "T" in that previous sentence! Maybe *that's* why it's broken!

Sometimes, I have to push the key down a bit so it works again or hit it a few times or it just doesn't work and there are no letter "Ts" in my previous sentence and I have to go back and put them in.

Yet here I am. Typing, using the letter T, plugged into an outlet, on some ancient OS, and banging out a chapter anyway.

Anyway.

No matter what.

I'm just going to do it.

I'm doing it.

I'm done.

Dear Reader,

If you are possibly saying, "Oh sure, Bradley, it's easy for you to say all of this stuff because you wrote for 2,808 days in a row. Blah blah blah."

Please know I'm writing this as much for you as I am for me.

I stopped my 2,808-day streak on the day my mom passed away and I haven't started another streak since.

I miss it. I need it.

It's like brushing your teeth. You don't say, "Well, I brushed my teeth really well last year so I don't have to this year."

You keep going. Forever. Because you know it's good for you. Because, afterwards, you'll appreciate it. Your entire day will benefit from this half hour I spent backspacing and fixing many of my letter "T" mistakes along the way.

I'm going to quote one of my favorite subtitles yet again.

Decide. There's usually a choice. It's usually yours.

It's simple. Oh so simple.

It's just not always easy.

- **Possible:** bring your good laptop
- **Impossible:** create with what you don't have
- **Repossible:** use what you have

I'll put a photo of my keyboard in the bonus content.

28

CREATE FOR ME

A SUCCESS BEFORE I WRITE IT, BEFORE ANYONE READS IT

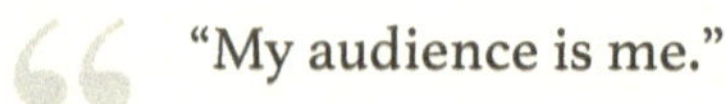 "My audience is me."

— ME (OR, WELL, YOU)

One of the main reasons this book came into existence was because of a book titled "You Must Write a Book." One of my issues with that book and that title is when you ask yourself who the audience of that book is or the reason you're writing it—or feel you must.

If you are of the opinion that you must or at least should write a book, who would you be writing it for? For a specific audience? Maybe a future audience? Fans that don't yet exist? Or maybe you hope they will come if or when you write the book?

There are lots of if's and when's in there.

I'm going to again quote from our Easiest Book Ever author who, before she even wrote her book, only when she thought of the idea of the book, when the title came to her, did she already succeed. She succeeded so quickly and so convincingly because she was her own audience. She was writing her book for her.

Did you catch that part where she was a success before she even wrote the book?

I feel the urge for a numbered list to highlight this point.

She was a success:

1. Before she wrote the book
2. Before anyone read the book

It was simply (and yet also extremely powerfully) the **idea** for the book that propelled her into her success.

Here's the difference between you (1) must write a book, you (2) should write a book, and you're (3) ready and willing to write a book.

That last one is when you get to the point where you feel you *can't not* write the book. You want to, you feel it, you then need to (but only out of your own need) and you must write it (again, only because you feel you must).

See the difference? Feel the difference?

Create for creating sake. Create for me. (Not the Bradley me, but the you me.)

- **Possible:** create for someone
- **Impossible:** create for everyone
- **Repossible:** create for me

Bonus Content: I turned on the camera and hit record which gave me the content, the idea, the drive and the meaning to then come and write this chapter. Remember, I firstly call myself a writer. However, recently I am more and more hitting record to get the idea straight in my head, to run through it, *to edit it by recording it*, to then know what I needed to write. Find the video, recorded on the island of Hydra in Greece here: go.repossible.com/ydht-bonus. Look for the lesson called "Create for Me."

Bonus Takeaway Quote from the Video: "There's no way I can fail." I called it an experiment so the only result is something learned.

Even if I learned that the answer is no or don't do that or that chapter is a bad idea, I learned something from it. There is no way to fail. How about that when you're starting an action? There is no way this could fail.

PART VII

SO DON'T

IT'S FINE. I'M FINE. IT'S FINE.

"There are risks and costs to action. But they are far less than the long range risks of comfortable inaction."

— JOHN F. KENNEDY

29

TOMORROW, TOMORROW, TOMORROW

YESTERDAY IS GONE, TOMORROW WILL NEVER ARRIVE, THERE IS ONLY TODAY

 "Never put off till tomorrow what you can do the day after tomorrow."

— MARK TWAIN

Nine years. At the beginning of that time is when I wish I had read this book to have given me a roadmap, a treasure map, of what to do, how to do it, why, and when.

Of course, at the beginning of that time I probably wouldn't have seen it or understood it or even if I had, probably wouldn't have acted upon it.

I spent about nine years thinking over, dreaming about, "working on," and not actually becoming a writer.

It quietly both kept me going (by dreaming of my future self) and tortured me (because I wasn't there yet).

I wasn't actually taking any concrete action (like, you know, actually writing) towards my goal, my dream, my future self.

I was just thinking about it.

I was *dreaming the dream* instead of *living the life*.

I didn't have a plan, a roadmap, a treasure map with a path and a timeline to get there.

This book could ideally give you a plan that you could accomplish in under 17 hours. From 4:00 in the afternoon to 9:00 the next morning.

17 Hours

17 hours from right now. Or from this afternoon. Or tomorrow afternoon.

That's when you could take real action and turn that vague idea of tomorrow (or worse: someday) into today.

Here's the treasure map in its simplest form:

1. **Fast:** stop eating today at 4 PM
2. **Meditate:** sit for between 20 and 40 minutes right after you wake up
3. **Create:** write down or record (audio or video) your treasures

I repeat it here to remind you (and to remind me) how easy it can be.

17 hours.

Bonus: Do it a few days in a row.

Double Bonus: prolong the fasting period.

If you're reading this before 3 PM, you can start today.

Fun Fact: Did you know when you start today that tomorrow vanishes?

- **Possible:** tomorrow
- **Impossible:** yesterday
- **Repossible:** today

30

MUDDY, MEEK, AND MISTRUST
THIS IS WHAT HAPPENS WHEN YOU DON'T

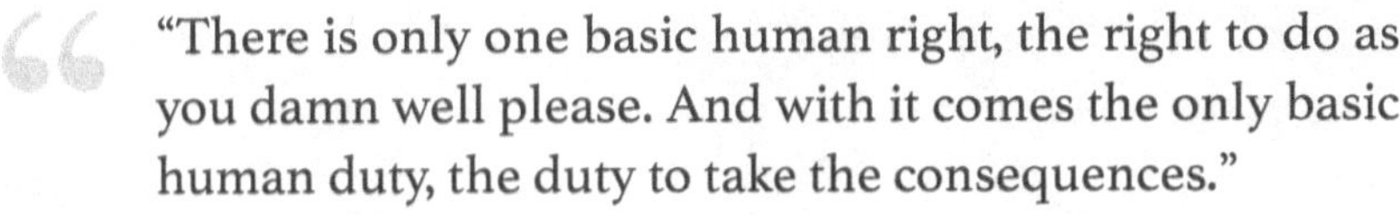

"There is only one basic human right, the right to do as you damn well please. And with it comes the only basic human duty, the duty to take the consequences."

— P. J. O'ROURKE

It's Wednesday morning. 9:00 AM.

I have an alternative path and I was trying to think of (witty) words to describe how that's going.

Instead of:

- Clarity
- Courage
- Confidence

I'm feeling more:

- Muddy
- Meek
- Mistrust

My wife and I had a super fun weekend: out late, went to a concert (Barbara Pravi was awesome!), ate lots, drank lots, to sleep late, up late.

I didn't really have a place for my meditation (nor the energy as I slept so late).

> "Ah well, I'm on a mini-vacation. I can skip a day, right!?"

I brush my teeth on my mini-vacation.

So can I not skip a meditation, am I allowed to eat (too much) dinner and have a Hefe Weizen, go to bed late, and not meditate in the morning, sitting properly in a chair for 23 minutes of my favorite guided meditation of the week?

Has it come to that?

Is that what I have to choose?

One or the other?

No.

I honest and truly don't want to be the person who, at the dinner party, proclaims loudly:

> "Oh, _________? *(Insert ANY food you actually like.)* You all still eat that? I gave that up long ago. I would never torture my body with such poison."
>
> — PERSON I NEVER WANT TO BE

Yet even with my witty title giving you an out, a legitimate reason to NOT have to do a thing, of course, quietly, maybe subconsciously, I am saying that probably you should do the thing.

Also, don't forget, we create most often for ourselves (no, really, it's true). So I'm trying to give myself my own get out of jail free card so I don't have to go on a mini-vacation and bore my wife to death when I don't eat dinner, have water instead, don't drink alcohol (see dinner menu = water), go to bed at 9 PM, wake up at 5 AM, meditate in a chair for a good hour, and then have a great day.

Except for that part that I'd be doing this all ... alone. Because she would be away on a weekend with girlfriends who, you know, actually have some fun.

 "But fasting and meditating and creating IS fun, darling!"

— HOPEFULLY NEVER ME

Let me remind myself and you, dear reader, of the title of this chapter. **Muddy, Meek, and Mistrust.**

Let me add some fuel to the fire and remind myself that I'm not feeling 100% either. I'm sniffly and stuffed up.

I smile as I write this because this chapter has somehow become a discussion, a heated argument between me and myself.

 "Well, Mr. Party Dude, I bet that you're not feeling great because you didn't fast, meditate, and create this weekend!"

— MY ALTER EGO IN I-TOLD-YOU-SO VOICE

Just a few years ago, I'm pretty sure that if I had to decide between eating, partying, and "enjoying life" in that way or to choose a life of fasting, meditating, and creating, the former would have won out.

Today, if I could truly only choose one, I would choose the latter.

Yet, dear reader, herein lies the beauty: we don't have to choose. We can have both worlds.

The You Don't Have To element of this chapter is that we don't have to only do the eating, drinking, partying mode. It's one of our options. We can choose to do it when we feel like it.

But as the quote at the top of this chapter reminds us, we live with the consequences.

 "There's usually a choice. It's usually yours."

— SUBTITLE OF "DECIDE"

Of course, the answer to all of this is balance. How much of which and when?

Even though I'm still not feeling great 671 words into this chapter, I can fully say with confidence that I feel better than when I started. No fasting, no meditating, just creating.

Even one element of the three is better than no element of the three.

- **Possible:** don't
- **Impossible:** don't (and say you did)
- **Repossible:** don't (and compare with when you do)

PART VIII

ELEVATE

ACTIVATE, CELEBRATE, ELEVATE

"Only passions, great passions can elevate the soul to great things."

— DENIS DIDEROT

31

WHAT GETS MEASURED GETS IMPROVED

RECORD, DOCUMENT, GET IT OUT (OF YOUR HEAD)

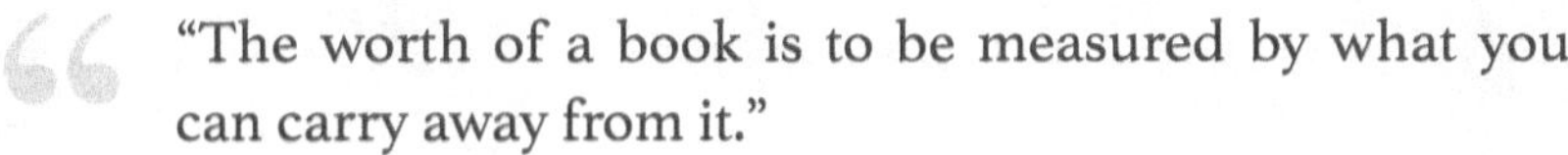

"The worth of a book is to be measured by what you can carry away from it."

— JAMES BRYCE

I have two teenage boys in high school. I've studied quite a bit about how to study. Short-term memory and long-term memory. Retention. All that. Oh, and teenagers. Who don't really care so much about the topic and are mostly there because they have to be.

What was the title of this book again?

So, sure, they're going to forget the math formula as soon as possible after the exam. Oh well.

But what about us?

Fasting, meditating, and creating.

I know my kids understand the material when they can "teach" it back to us. We have a discussion about it, we ask questions and they respond as best they know.

That's the best. The worst is when they skim or read and barely comprehend the material.

See where I'm going with this?

Sure, I'm almost certain you'll benefit from a 17-hour session of fasting, meditating, and creating.

But if we add some measurement to the equation, it usually sticks with us longer, has a deeper, more profound learning experience.

How can we measure if we don't have any system of currency or something to measure?

The simple example is always weight loss. If you lost weight, you'll know it because the scale shows a smaller number than last week. Super easy to measure—and improve.

In fact, at least for me, weight loss or at least weight management, is an important measurement factor in the three-part equation. I feel better (harder to measure) when I weigh less (easier to measure).

Aside from weight loss, most of what we're doing here is harder to measure.

Let's take just the three main elements:

- Clarity
- Courage
- Confidence

How do we know, week to week or month to month, that we have more of those things?

This is where recording or documenting comes in. For a few months now, I have been recording a post-meditation audio. I'm no less than amazed at what comes through during those less-than-10-minute sessions.

A few short years ago, those recordings would have been secured in the deepest password-protected folders of my Dropbox. But, seeing that I have now apparently completely come out of the spiritual closet, I not only record them but I then publish them publicly. I know, it's crazy. You can listen to them here: passthesourcream.com/tag/past-life-regressions/.

By recording a quick audio snippet of the recap of my meditation, it embeds it deeper within me. It helps me remember it longer and

I'm pretty sure it also subconsciously engrains it more profoundly in the section of my brain labeled something like "experiences that are apparently important to me."

By recording, by taking notes, by telling yourself and your mind and your brain and your, well, soul, that what you're doing is important, it will become more important for you and thus it will be more deeply embedded in yourself.

I hope I'm getting this message across clearly.

If you're looking for the action item, in case it got buried in here somewhere, it's just this:

> *ACTION: Immediately after your meditation (or creating session), hit voice record on your phone and just talk through what just happened. Keep it under 10 minutes. Save that file in a place where you can see your progress if only by the number of recordings you have.*
>
> *TECH TIP: I personally use Voice Record Pro on my iPhone. There should be an app on your phone that's already installed you can also use. I like VRP because I can easily export it to Dropbox.*

You know in books where there are exercises in the chapters and the authors will even say something like, "Now, go do the exercise. I'll wait!" Yep, that's what I'm saying here, too.

It's the same thing as doing your meditation and not recording it. Yep, it was probably good, but it will be enhanced if you record, if you measure how good it was.

I can sense in myself a need for an answer to the question, "But Bradley, how often should I record what—and why?" Which is why I need to go write the next chapter of this book called Frequency.

- **Possible:** record your experience without actually hitting record
- **Impossible:** think about it in your head as if that's as good as actively recording your voice or your words on paper

- **Repossible:** just hit record

P.S. Remember, I'm a rebel and a nutty professor who does crazy stuff like this and then publicly shares it. I honestly don't recommend this when you're starting out. Yes, hit record, but it's just for you and only you. That way, you'll also be more honest and daring to really, really get into how your experience went.

32

FREQUENCY

HOW OFTEN TO DO WHAT—AND WHY

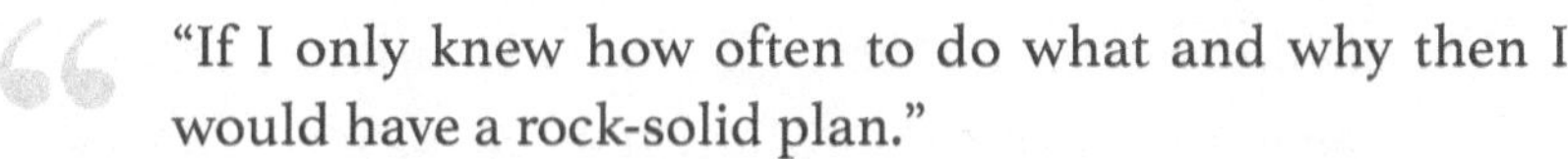

> "If I only knew how often to do what and why then I would have a rock-solid plan."
>
> — BRADLEY CHARBONNEAU (PAST AND PRESENT)

I'm writing this chapter quite late in the game with this book. As I realize what this book has become (an actionable treasure map with repeatable results) I'm already anticipating questions from you—because I already have them myself.

Here's one I had/still have:

> "So Bradley, yeah, so this fasting and meditating and creating stuff all sounds great. I'm in. But whew. How often do I do what?"
>
> — ME & MAYBE YOU

Here's my short answer: find your own frequency.

Here's my long answer: here's what I do so you can have an

example to start with and then adjust according to what works best for you.

> *PSA: This topic, frequency, is so ridiculously important to me I thought about making an entire series about it with titles such as Every Single Day (already written), Every Single Week and then Month, Year, and Lifetime. I don't know if I'll do the full series but maybe it's just a single book called Frequency with those time frames as parts/sections. Stay tuned!*

Here's my current frequency as regards to fasting, meditating, and creating.

- **Hourly:** Breathing. Deep breath in through the nose. Exhale through the mouth. A conscious breath. You know the difference. Bonus? Hear your breath going out. (Time: maybe 5 seconds)
- **Daily:**
- a.) Meditate. 17 minutes to 51 minutes, depending on how early I'm awake, how I'm feeling, and what time Luca has to go to school.
- b.) Creating. Writing, recording (audio or video), even a photo or a single note taken in a notebook. But *something*.
- **Weekly:**
- a.) Past life regression meditation (Friday mornings).
- b.) 17-hour fasting (Thursday evenings).
- c.) Thursday Thunder, weekly video episodes.
- (d.) Zoom masterminds.
- **Monthly:**
- a.) Meditation group in person.
- b.) Email newsletter "The 17th." (Yep, I have my favorite numbers and ritualize them.)
- **Quarterly:** Group event. In person.

- **Annually:** Bigger group event (retreat, workshop, ideally out of my own country).
- **Lifetime:** Host an event.

Wow, that took me longer than I thought!

> *PRO TIP: When something flows and you feel you need more time because there's so much good stuff in there, it might be a sign that you need to do more on that topic. Here it's clearly a sign that I need to get working on the book Frequency.*

Too much information above?
How about a short version:

1. Meditate daily
2. Fast weekly
3. Create weekly

Adjust to your own frequency. Then wash, rinse, repeat.

Oh, and don't forget the previous chapter, "What Gets Measured Gets Improved" as that is actually the **Secret Sauce to success for all of this.**

You're not going to get the real answers from this book. Just like a map only shows you how to get from A to B, you're going to have to put on the shoes and step outside the door—and probably step outside your comfort zone.

- **Possible:** guess your frequency
- **Impossible:** match your exact frequency to someone else
- **Repossible:** find your frequency

33

CHERISH THE CHASE

OF IF YOU PREFER OVERUSED CLICHÉS, IT'S THE JOURNEY, NOT THE DESTINATION

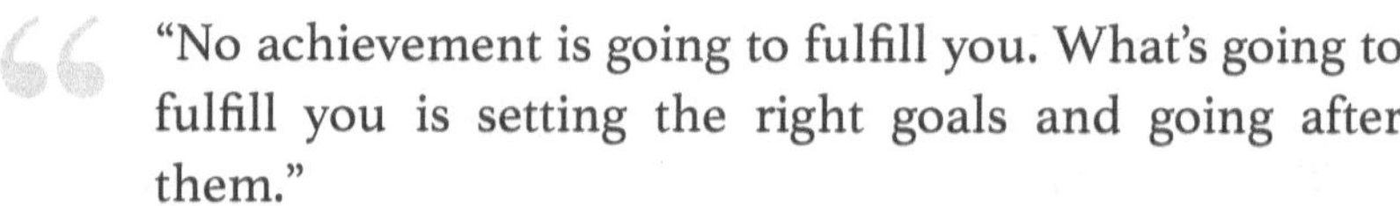

"No achievement is going to fulfill you. What's going to fulfill you is setting the right goals and going after them."

— BRAD STULBERG

A friend in my mastermind group shared an article with me that explained a common phenomenon in such clear and simple terms, it hit home deep and hard.

The article was about some famous athletes who, after winning or succeeding in a huge way, it was followed by a dip, even a depression that they didn't expect. Until it happened again after the next big high.

Big giant peak followed by deep valley.

I'm not a huge fan of the word journey and I'm even less a fan of the phrase, It's the Journey, Not the Destination, although it's true and I'm a big believer.

A monumental challenge to this whole premise is because ... it's hard. It's difficult. It's not as fun to cherish the bus ride as it is to celebrate when you arrive.

The journey, the ride, the practice, the rituals, the daily grind, is usually less about fireworks and more about ... work.

What I especially appreciate about Brad Stulberg's article is that it doesn't just suggest you simply enjoy the getting there but he says we need to set the right goals and go after them.

See how much more active that is? Even pro-active?

I'm feeling the need for a numbered list because it's simple and powerful—yet not easy to implement.

1. Set (the right) goals
2. Go after them

To apply the article to this book, I can only hope that it came through how much joy and pleasure and meaning and fulfillment I get from doing a single night of fasting, of going through even the "normal" meditations, and then writing a single chapter.

Sure, the fireworks and lightning strikes are fun but the marathon runner has to get something out of the daily practice and not only wait for the marathon to enjoy it, to get something out of it, to cherish the chase.

And remember, we're talking about activities here that can be a whole lot more fun than running. Fasting, meditation, and creating can offer up destinations that we hadn't even expected.

That element, the unknown, the unexpected, is why I do the daily routines. If I knew exactly what would happen each time, if it was the same as running and I did the same 5 K each day along the same path with the same outcome each time, I'd probably go crazy.

But knowing that I don't know what's coming?

I have goals, both small and big, and I need to be OK with not quite knowing or even caring about how I'll actually get there. I just put in the steps, put in the work, stick to the system, the treasure map, and I'll eventually get there.

That's setting the goals and going after them. That's cherishing the chase.

- **Possible:** enjoy the journey and the destination
- **Impossible:** enjoy the destination before you get there
- **Repossible:** cherish the chase

The link to the article is in the bonus content under the lesson title Cherish the Chase.

34

SPIRAL UP

IT'S GOING TO BE A SPIRAL. WE CAN CHOOSE WHETHER IT GOES UP OR DOWN.

"I see clarity and courage and confidence as a circle. Or better yet, a spiral. But not a downward spiral, an upward spiral. Spiral up."

— DR. KAYVON K.

One of the benefits of being an author is you can talk about the topics of your book and then quote people and ask them if it's OK if you quote them and put them in your book.

I was just on a Zoom call for my entrepreneur mastermind group and I briefly mentioned this book and Dr. Kayvon K. quickly saw his own version of clarity and courage and confidence.

Even if you say "I'm working on a book" (which I usually joke about because everyone says they're working on a book which usually translates into "I'm working on a book but not actually working on but thinking about and oh I'll probably never actually write it") people will usually want to know about it.

PRO TIP: Keep it short! This entire chapter came into exis-

> *tence because I spent less than two minutes talking
> about this book's title and main message. Not two
> hours. Not two days. Two minutes.*

So you talk about it. You invite their opinion. It might turn into nothing. People like being invited to things.

Think about these *invitations*:

1. "Could I get your feedback on my book?"
2. "Would you like to edit my manuscript?"
3. "I like your ideas on topic X. Could I interview you on my podcast?"

Are you more excited by one over the other? Frankly, at least for me, here's how I would react:

1. "Are you buying dinner?"
2. "Would you like me to remove your teeth with pliers?"
3. "Wow, I'd be honored. Name a time and I'll be there."

Spiral Up

We're better together.

Although you could (and should) experience this book and execute the actions alone, we can only grow so much on our own.

See how this chapter came into existence? I shared my idea (it was literally as simple as mentioning the title, *You Don't Have To*, and then the idea that the book will give you more clarity, courage, and confidence) and my friend had a quick and clear vision of how he saw it and he shared it with me.

Literally while we were on our Zoom call, I multitasked and created just the title of this chapter and his quote.

I also asked him, "Hey Kayvon, can I use that quote in my book?"

Think for a moment how this is *Spiraling Up* in action.

I didn't ask him a big favor, I didn't even directly ask his opinion of my title or my main message. I just put it out there in the open and let him respond. Remember, he might not have responded at all and that's OK, too. In fact, on that note, if they don't respond, let it go. Don't push it, don't worry about it. But keep sharing and seeing with whom you resonate, let them respond, and invite them as a guest on your podcast, ask if you can quote them, and spiral up the conversation.

Now take this idea and apply it to fasting, meditating, and creating. You could do it once in a while and things will probably improve.

But what if you take that *linear* improvement and you turn it into a *spiraling up*?

You talk about your experiences with others. You record (audio or video) your experience with one or all of the elements of the practice. It could be as simple as an audio recording that started out as "I just got out of my meditation. Here's what happened."

If you don't record your progress, you tend to miss out on the possible exponential gains from measuring. Some marketing guru said something like, "What gets measured gets improved."

> *Meta Note from the Author: this chapter, inspired by*
> *Kayvon, has led me to another new chapter about*
> *measuring and recording and documenting. See how*
> *that works? This is again spiraling up in real-life action.*

Share your experiences with others (briefly!). See if they respond. Write down or record your experiences.

- **Possible:** clarity and courage and confidence as a straight line alone
- **Impossible:** spiraling up as fast or efficiently or effectively alone as together with others
- **Repossible:** spiral up together exponentially

P.S. Dr. Kayvon K. also mentioned this quote below which could also happen if you ask people to edit your manuscript (or listen to you talk about fasting or meditating). You think you're asking for a little thing, you assume you might even be inviting them to something fun or exciting or rewarding, you're just trying to fix their eyebrow and you (accidentally) blind them.

 "I tried to fix his eyebrow and I blinded him."

— FARSI SAYING

ABOUT THE AUTHOR

I used to think we had to do things. Sure, death and taxes. But many other things.

But we don't.

I have a chapter in my book Every Single Day called "The Conundrum of Comfortable." It's one of my favorite chapters.

It's about how if we didn't grow up in a war zone or with a terrible dictator or _________ (fill in the blank of other and very possible horrible living situation that exists) but if our problems are, as we say in the first world, "First-World Problems," then sometimes we find ourselves in The Conundrum of Comfortable.

If we don't have to walk four miles with a water jug on our heads to get water but our "problems" are more along the lines of which milk we buy, then we can easily fall into The Conundrum of Comfortable.

Just like the three main topics of this book: writing a book, meditating, and intermittent fasting.

I don't have to do *any* of them.

I want to do them.

I want to do all three of them.

I have done them (with great success and joy) and want to share those with you.

If you want to.

Not if you think you have to.

That's why I wrote this book.

I hope you enjoyed it.

I'm not really joking in the book about how I can't help you with fasting other than suggesting you stop eating at 4 PM and I don't really want to be your meditation guru (other than suggesting a few people I follow) although one place I might be able to help more directly is in writing a book.

I had a program last year called "How to Write Your Worst Book Ever" but people kept coming to me, during the program, saying, "Bradley, I really like and understand your goal of using this "worst book ever" as a tool to break through my procrastination or perfectionism but I've now already done that and even though you warned me not to, I'm working on my Best Book Ever. What do I do now?"

I changed the name of the program to "How to Write Your Easiest Book Ever" and there's a do-it-yourself version you can do with online lessons or there's a workshop group option I've been running twice a year that's been a huge success—and barrels of fun.

If you think you have a book in you (ha, that's a joke because I know we ALL have a book in us) but you'd actually like to take action and transfer that idea in your head to words on a page in a fast, reliable, and proven system, come join How to Write Your Easiest Book Ever and either DIY or DWY (Do It Yourself or Done With You) at go.repossible.com/ebe and use the coupon code YDHT for 25% off.

I currently live in a little town outside of Utrecht in The Netherlands with my wife Saskia, famous two young boys of "The Adventures of Li & Lu" fame, and our at-least-as-famous dog, Pepper.

This is my thirty-second book.

It is far, far, far from my last.

Find, ask, discuss, play, and dare at:
bradleycharbonneau.com or repossible.com

facebook.com/bradley.charbonneau.author
x.com/brathocha
instagram.com/brathocha

THE END

No, really.
      It's over.
      You don't have to.
Unless you really, really want to.

ALSO BY BRADLEY CHARBONNEAU

Most of my books are also available as audiobooks (which I giddily narrate).
Search for my name at your favorite audiobook distributor, slip on your
headphones, and let me take you away.

Repossible

Who Will You Be Next?

1. Repossible
2. Every Single Day (+ Playbook)
3. Ask
4. Dare
5. Create (also available: Box Set #1)
6. Decide
7. Meditate
8. Spark (also available: Box Set #2)
9. Surrender
10. Play
11. Celebrate (also available: Box Set #3 and Box Set Complete)
12. Frequency

Create

Inspired Action to Create the Next Chapter of Your Life

1. 17 Hours
2. How to Write Your Worst Book Ever
3. The One-Word-Long Book that Will Probably Change Your Life
4. I Love _____
5. Audio for Authors
6. Chapter Won
7. Book in a Weekend

8. One

9. Boost Your Brand with a Book

Impossible

A Parody of S(h)elf Help

1. Procrastinate

2. Waffle

Charlie Holiday

The Chance is Yours

1. Now Is Your Chance

2. Second Chance

3. Chance of a Lifetime (also available: Box Set)

Short Trips

Just Put on the Shoes

1. Secret Bus to Paradise

2. Where I (Already) Am

3. Pass the Sour Cream

4. A Trip to Hel

5. Goddamn Attitude

6. Drive-By Dropping

Li & Lu

Bring Adventure Home

1. The Secret of Kite Hill

2. The Secret of Markree Castle

3. The Key to Markree Castle

4. The Gift of Markree Castle
5. Driehoek (also available: Box Set)

Really Old ...

urban travel guide SAN FRANCISCO

* 9 7 9 8 2 0 1 1 0 5 5 6 3 *